Understanding
The Mother of Jesus

Understanding
The Mother of Jesus

EAMON R. CARROLL, O. Carm.

Michael Glazier, Inc.
Wilmington, Delaware

First Published in 1979 by
MICHAEL GLAZIER, INC.
1210A King Street
Wilmington, DE 19801

and

VERITAS PUBLICATIONS
7-8 Lower Abbey Street
Dublin 1, Ireland

Library of Congress Catalog Card Number: 78-74942
International Standard Book Number: 0-89453-101-8

Printed in the United States of America

Contents

FOREWORD

THIS BOOK reckons up some of the great gains in understanding the Mother of Jesus that have come about in recent
years through dedicated scholarship. The first part considers
four areas of development: scriptural insights; Mary, model
of the Church, as illustrated in the liturgy; Our Lady and
the Holy Spirit; ecumenical hopes. The second main section
is the transcript of a newspaper interview on the occasion of
the Marian Congress held in Sydney, Australia, September,
1976.

A full-scale study on the Blessed Virgin Mary is beyond
the scope of the present publication; the abundance and
variety of the books, articles, pamphlets and portions of
books in the Recommended Readings that make up Part III
of the book indicate how rich a field of exploration awaits
the serious reader about the Mother of God. Not only
Catholic writers but other Christians as well are devoting
respectful attention to the Mother of the Lord in her relationship to Christ and the Church. The author's hope is to open
doors, to indicate lines of further inquiry, to stimulate interest in the Mother of Jesus as a lively and joyful theological
theme.

John Henry Newman's last sermon at Oxford University
as an Anglican was on our Lady's faith (February 2, 1843).
His first book of sermons as a Catholic contained two on
our Lady (*Discourses Addressed to Mixed Congregations,*
1849): "The glories of Mary for the Sake of her Son," and
"On the fitness of the glories of Mary," which includes the
following sentences: "Her glories are not only for the sake
of her Son, they are for our sakes also." "She has no chance
place in the Divine Dispensation . . . He is the Wisdom of

God, she is therefore the Seat of Wisdom: His Presence is Heaven, she therefore is the Gate of Heaven; He is infinite Mercy, she then is the Mother of Mercy."

The year of Pope Paul VI's death, Edward D. O'Connor, C.S.C., published *Pope Paul and the Spirit. Charisms and Church Renewal in the Teaching of Paul VI* (Notre Dame, Indiana, 1978). The analysis of statements on the Blessed Virgin and the Holy Spirit from the fifteen years of Pope Paul's pontificate is in the chapter, "The Sacraments, the Hierarchy and the Virgin Mary." These topics are characteristic of Catholic understanding of the Church; they rest on the principle the Holy Spirit makes use of human realities to channel his gifts. In a foreword to O'Connor's book Cardinal Suenens notes "the necessary connection between charism and hierarchy, charism and sacramental life, charism and devotion to Mary . . . the future of the Charismatic Renewal as well as its fruitfulness . . . depend, so far as Catholics are concerned, on . . . being deeply rooted in the Church. Concretely, this means their acceptance of the *magisterium* of Peter and of the spiritual motherhood of Mary. Christ was born of Mary and the Holy Spirit, and this indissoluble association remains a vital one."

Representing the Presbyterian tradition, Dr. J.A. Ross Mackenzie took part in the June, 1973, program at the Catholic University of America, Washington, D.C., *The Virgin Mary in Ecumenical Perspective,* lecturing on "The Mother of God in Reformed Piety." He put the question, "What does it mean in our day to proclaim Mary blessed and to find her place in the liturgy and prayer of the Church?" Part of his reply was, "God calls mankind to the fulness of which Jesus Christ is the revelation and means and goal. Mary was the first to respond to this call, and she remains the sign and stimulus of our praise of God. And as Luther said, 'To praise the Lord with gladness is not a human work.' "

In his greatest Marian document, *Marialis cultus,* "for the right ordering and development of devotion to the Blessed Virgin Mary" (February 2, 1974), Pope Paul VI explained his purpose, "to remove doubts, and, especially, to help the development of that devotion to the Blessed Virgin which is motivated in the Church by the Word of God and practised in the Spirit of Christ." His successor Pope John Paul I opened his pontificate with similar expressions of confidence in the loving care of the Blessed Virgin, holy Mother of Christ. The hopes expressed on both Reformed and Catholic sides are the goals of *Understanding the Mother of Jesus.*

The final note is a word of thanks to Alan Gill, for his provocative questions in the Australian interview (Part II); Father Alfred Boeddeker, O.F.M., and the staff of the St. Boniface Marian Centre, San Francisco, for constant help; Patrice Stolz and Mary Ann Robert for secretarial assistance; and the Sisters of Mercy of Russell College, Burlingame, California, who provided the refuge for the writing work.

Part I: Significant New Developments in the Study of the Blessed Virgin

The Mother of Jesus and the Scriptures

THE MOST promising area for deeper understanding of the Mother of Jesus is the Scriptures. Catholic biblical scholarship has flowered in recent decades, especially since the 1943 letter by Pope Pius XII on the promotion of scriptural studies, The biblical approach of the Vatican Council's consideration of our Lady had ecumenical as well as catechetical and pastoral importance.

An example of the new insights is the Council's use of the so-called "difficult sayings" from the public life, the incidents of the true kinsmen (Mark 3, Matthew 12, Luke 8) and the enthusiastic woman (Luke 11). For over a century Roman documents on our Lady, e.g., the ten rosary encyclicals of Pope Leo XIII, shied away from these texts, apparently afraid they would be used as arguments against Catholic devotion to Mary. The Council read both incidents in the sense of praise of the Mother of Jesus.

The event related only by St. Luke (ch. 11, 27-28) tells of the woman who shouts out from the crowd, praising Jesus by praising his mother, "Blessed is the womb that bore you and the breasts that nursed you" (like Proverbs 10, 1; 23, 25), to win from Jesus the reply, "Still more blessed are those who hear the word of God and keep it." As Fr. Raymond Brown has written recently, studying the place of Mary in these most ancient Gospel materials, the first features of Jesus' mission and message to be preached in the young Church, an influence can be traced from the implied praise of Jesus' mother in her Son's reply to the unknown woman from the crowd to the words of Mary herself at the Annunciation, "Behold the handmaid of the Lord; be it done unto me according to your word."

The words of Elizabeth to her young cousin Mary when she visits her, the familiar rosary mystery and liturgical feast of the Visitation (May 31, formerly July 2), are similar also to the woman's praise in the public life, for Elizabeth says, "Blessed are you among women and blessed is the fruit of your womb." Jesus answered the woman's praise with: "Still more blessed are those who hear the word of God and keep it." Like Jesus, Elizabeth, filled with the Holy Spirit, goes beyond the simple praise of the anonymous woman, to praise Mary for the faith in which her motherhood is rooted; her words form the first beatitude in the gospels, "Blessed is she who has believed, for the things promised her by the Lord will be accomplished in her" (New Oxford Annotated).

The other incident, the one story mentioning Mary common to the synoptics, found in all three, St. Mark, St. Matthew and St. Luke, is the account of the "true kinsmen." If we put the question, "What place had the Mother of Jesus in the earliest Christian preaching?" the answer is this incident of the true kinsmen. The familiar circumstances are that the mother and the relatives (the biblical "brethren" or "brothers and sisters") come on the scene while Jesus is preaching. Word is sent him that they wish to speak to him. As St. Mark, oldest version of the story, relates it, a sharp distinction is made between those who are listening to Jesus, the "insiders" seated around him, and the relatives, who are "outside." The tone of the Savior's reply in St. Mark is severe, "Who are my mother and my brothers?. . . These are my mother and my brothers. Whoever does the will of God is brother and sister and mother to me." (Mk 3 33-5).

St. Luke makes some striking modifications in the true kinsmen story; he tells the anecdote in such a way that the Mother of Jesus appears as the perfect example of hearing the word of God and keeping it. "My mother and my brothers are those who hear the word of God and act upon it" (Luke 8, 21). Chapter eight of St. Luke begins with the parable of the sower; the concluding line of Jesus' explanation is, "The seed on good ground are those who hear the word of God in a spirit of openness, retain it, and bear fruit through perseverance" (8, 15). Next comes the parable of the lamp, not hidden under a bushel basket or bed, but put high on a lampstand for all to see, with the advice, "Take heed, therefore, how you hear . . ."

St. Luke has made the incident of the true kinsmen the conclusion of a series of teachings of Jesus about hearing the word of God: the parable of the sower, the parable of the lamp, and then the story of the coming of the mother and the brethren. The Virgin Mary is the "blessed" one before all others, the woman of noble and generous heart who heard the word and took it to herself, and yielded the great harvest through her perseverance, through her love and faith, above all through her union with Christ. When St. Mark and St. Matthew wind up the story of the true kinsmen, they report Jesus as saying, "Whoever does the will of my Father . . ." St. Luke has Jesus say rather, "My mother and my brothers are those *who hear the word of God* and act upon it." For St. Luke the Virgin Mary, Mother of Jesus, is the outstanding example of openness to the word of God, of receptivity to God's grace. As Fr. Brown has written, "Luke has developed a major interest in Mary as the first disciple who heard the word of God and did it (1:38); she was present at the beginning of the Gospel and at the beginning of the Church (Acts 1:14)" *(The Catholic Mind,* June, 1977). On the occasion of the gathering in the upper room, before Pentecost, in the Acts of the Apostles, St. Luke again places among the true followers of the Lord the relatives of Jesus, naming his mother. After listing the apostles he writes, "All these with one accord devoted themselves to prayer, together with the women and Mary the mother of Jesus and with his brothers" (New Oxford Annotated, Acts 1; 14).

In spite of the hundred-year silence in Roman Marian documents about these incidents from the public life which mention Mary, the liturgy was never silent about them. The story of the enthusiastic woman has been in use for centuries as the gospel reading on our Lady's days (Luke 11, 27-28) and the story of the true kinsmen was also used in the Marian liturgy (Luke 8, 19-21).

Pope Paul VI repeated the old pattern of the liturgical readings, as well as appealing to the insights of the Second Vatican Council when he wrote in *Marialis cultus* of Mary as "first and most perfect of Christ's disciples . . . worthy of imitation . . . because she heard the word of God and acted upon it." "When the Church's children unite their voices with the voice of the unknown woman in the Gospel and glorify the Mother of Jesus by saying to him. 'Blessed is the womb that bore thee, and the breasts that nursed thee,' they will be led to ponder the divine Master's serious reply, 'Rather blessed are they who hear the word of God and keep it' — a reply that is both lively praise of Mary . . . and also an admonition for us to live our lives in accordance with God's commandments" (no. 39).

The opening chapters of St. Matthew and St. Luke which deal with the infancy and childhood of Jesus are the reflection of the early Church on the meaning of Jesus and his mission. The oldest gospel materials are the public life of the Savior, culminating in the passion, death and resurrection. The evangelical accounts of the infancy and childhood of Jesus were composed not principally as biographical narratives but with the doctrinal purpose of bringing out the meaning of Jesus as Messiah and Redeemer. Such recent books as Fr. R. E. Brown's *The Birth of the Messiah* (Garden City, N.Y., 1977) show the marvelous complexity of the familiar stories of the annunciation, the visit to Elizabeth, the birth at Bethlehem, the presentation of the Christ-Child in the temple, and the finding of the 12-year old Jesus in the temple. In all these events the Mother of Jesus has part, and her place is filled with meaning for the Church. As St. Luke depicts Mary of Nazareth, virgin Mother of Jesus, she is the great gospel woman of faith, blessed because of her faith, in the infancy chapters even as in the public life incidents.

The sense of fulfillment of messianic prophecy and promise in Jesus is true also of his mother in the infancy chapters. The Council referred to Mary as "the exalted daughter of Sion in whom the times are fulfilled after the long waiting for the promise, and the new economy inaugurated when the Son of God takes on human nature from her in order to free men from sin by the mysteries of his flesh" *(Lumen gentium,* no. 55). In the Hebrew bible " daughter of Sion" referred to the people of God, often described as a woman, the bride of God. In Christian understanding, Mary of Nazareth is the individual daughter of Sion in whom the hopes of her people have come to perfection. "She stands out among the Lord's lowly and poor [the "anawim." Hebrew word for the poor people of God] who confidently look for salvation from him and receive it" (n.55).

Henri Cazalles, S.S., French Scripture expert who has served as president of the society of French scholars especially interested in the study of our Lady, and who has been guest professor frequently at the Catholic University of America in Washington, D.C., wrote a few years ago this reflection on Mary as the "daughter of Sion": "Without the Marian mystery, the apostolate would add up to an heroic world, like the Church of persecution times; with Mary, the daughter of Sion, who brings forth by the very action of God (Genesis 4, 1), the apostolate accomplishes still more than construction; it vivifies the universe and all creation in the growth of the great tree of parables and the body of the Pauline epistles."

St. Matthew and St. Luke bear witness to Mary's virginal motherhood of Jesus. The Savior is "conceived of the Holy Spirit, born of the Virgin Mary," without a human father, for the incarnation is a new creation. God accomplishes salvation independently of the normal laws of procreation, not by the will of the flesh, not by the will of man (John 1, 13), yet also not without the free consent of the Virgin Mary, willing and humble handmaid of the Lord. God shows his favor where he chooses, whether in barren Sara, the wife of Abraham of old, or elderly Elizabeth, the kinswoman of Mary, who becomes mother of John the Baptist in spite of Zachary's doubt, or in Mary the virgin, as Gabriel says, repeating the promise God made to Abraham, "for nothing is impossible to God" (Luke 1, 37 and Genesis 18, 14). St. Augustine saw Mary as the daughter of Abraham in her faith. Her faith made Mary great. No one was ever a more steadfast daughter in the faith of Abraham, "who believed and it was accounted to him for righteousness." The words of the Magnificat show Mary felt herself bound up with Abraham. She too believed in God's promise, she too experienced his mercy, "even as he promised our fathers, promised Abraham and his descendants for ever." Jews and Christians and Muslims too honor Abraham as our father in faith. On gospel evidence Christians can call Mary "our mother in faith, mother of believers."

In the last Gospel, St. John, the mother of Jesus is present twice only, at the beginning of her Son's ministry, the wedding feast of Cana, and again when his great hour has come, by the cross of Jesus on Calvary. On both occasions Jesus addresses her as "woman," on both occasions her presence is an aspect of the mysteries of Christ and the Church. At Cana Mary asks for wine, not merely an extra supply to save the wedding feast, but the wine of the new covenant, promised for messianic times. The change of water into wine is a sign of the blessings Jesus brings, from the weak water used for the Jewish religious purifications into the rich wine of the royal wedding between Christ and his bride the Church, for whom he will lay down his life when his "hour" comes. Mary is at the wedding feast as the "daughter of Sion," greeting the messianic bridegroom representing the Church, his bride.

On Calvary the Mother of Jesus stands by her Son's cross to hear him say, "Woman, behold your son," and to the beloved disciple, "Behold your mother" (John 19, 25-27). At the Last Supper Jesus had spoken to his followers of the pain-filled hour of giving birth, and then continued, "But when she has brought forth the child, she no longer remembers the anguish for her joy that a man is born into the world" (John 16, 21). The longing of Israel for the coming of the messianic age was compared to labor pains, and the daughter of Sion had been promised a progeny that would include all nations. The words of the dying, yet victorious, Christ from his cross proclaim the fulfillment of that promise, for Mary, the "woman," symbolizes mother Church, new Israel, mother of all human beings.

Another fascinating example of biblical scholarship providing an enriched appreciation of Mary is a recent study on the relationship between the Cana wedding in St. John's gospel and the Pentecost scene in the Acts of the Apostles.

A few years ago Dr. Joseph A. Grassi of Santa Clara University wrote a short study on Cana as a Pentecostal meditation (in the journal *Novum Testamentum,* April, 1972) and there is now in press a doctorate dissertation by the Italian Servite Aristide M. Serra, O.S.M., on "the contribution of ancient Jewish literature to the exegesis of John 2, 1-12 and John 19, 21-27," The following paragraphs are based on the findings of these scholars.

Christians took over the Jewish feast of Pentecost, which was originally a harvest celebration but by Jesus' day recalled also the giving of the Law, the Torah. The followers of Jesus celebrated Pentecost as the giving of the new Torah, through the resurrection of Christ and the sending of his Spirit. In the Acts the sound of a mighty wind, the tongues of fire, the voices understood in many languages are reminders of the covenant on Mt. Sinai. The resurrection of Jesus on the third day may relate to the third day on the mountain, signalizing the new covenant. As Grassi wrote, "In the symbolic sense of Jn ii, 3, the mother of Jesus appears to be a representative figure of the Church which implicitly asks for the new wine of the Spirit, as she says to Jesus, 'They have no wine.' In Acts i, 14 . . . Mary, the mother of Jesus, brethren and the twelve pray together for the gift of the Spirit. Corresponding to the wine at Cana, the effects of the Spirit are likened to those of new wine by the crowd when they remark, 'They are filled with new wine' (Acts ii, 13)." At Cana Jesus said to his mother, "My hour has not yet come." According to St. John's explanation the Spirit cannot be given until the hour of the death and glorification of Jesus. "Now this he said about the Spirit, which those who believed in him were to receive; for as yet the Spirit had not been given, because Jesus was not yet glorified" (John 7, 39).

Fr. Serra has explored in depth the Sinai significance of the sign of Cana, a meaning mentioned also by Pope Paul in

Marialis cultus, "The words of the Blessed Virgin Mary, 'Do whatever he tells you,' words which at first glance look like they are limited to the desire to remedy an embarrassment at the feast, seem in the context of St. John's gospel to be an echo of the words used by the people of Israel to give approval to the covenant on Mt. Sinai (see Ex 19, 8; 24, 3, 37; Dt 5, 27) and to renew their commitments (see Jos. 24, 24; Esd. 10, 12; Neh. 5, 12). And they harmonize wonderfully with the words spoken by the Father at the Mt. Tabor theophany: 'Hear him' (Mt 17, 5)" (no. 57).

On the exodus from Egypt the Israelites pitched camp at Sinai while Moses went up the mountain to meet God, who promised they would be a kingdom of priests, a holy nation, the people of the covenant. "When Moses set before them all that the Lord had ordered him to tell them, the people all answered together, 'Everything the Lord has said, we will do' " (Ex. 19, 7-8; Chapter 24 repeats their promise, again in Deut. 5, 7). In Exodus the Lord revealed himself to Moses on the third day, that the people might believe in him. "On the third day there was a marriage at Cana," "he let his glory be seen, and his disciples believed in him" (John 2, 1 and 12, beginning and end of the account). "As the gift of the Old Law was preceded by and made possible by the declaration of faith of all Israel, so the gift of the New Law, the Gospel of Christ, was preceded by and prepared for by the total self-giving of Mary to the will of her Son" (Serra). Israel was often described as a "woman" before God; using the title "woman" "Jesus sees in his mother the personification of Israel of old, now come to the fullness of time, to the days of the Messiah" (Serra).

At both Cana and Pentecost the result surpasses human expectation or possibility: the enormous amount of splendid wine, "filled to the brim," and at Pentecost, even as Jesus had promised, "It is not by measure that the Father gives the Spirit" (John 3, 34). In the Acts of the Apostles, the Spirit, symbolized by the abundant wine of Cana, "fills the house where they were gathered together" (2,2). "They were all filled with the Holy Spirit" (2,4), filled with new wine (2, 13), the great outpouring of the Spirit on all flesh reserved for the last days and prophesied by Joel, as St. Peter said in his Pentecost sermon.

The old wine has run out. The disciples, the brethren, the women present, and the mother of Jesus ask for the new wine of the Spirit, which is given through obedience to the word of Jesus as the nucleus of the new covenant. "Through Jesus, God gives the Spirit without measure to believers. Filled to the brim with the Spirit, they manifest his glory and bring the overflowing gift to others" (Grassi). Half a century ago Père Marie-Joseph Lagrange, the Dominican bible expert, reflected on similar lines, "This Son, who has the power of determining the hour of his own destiny, does not disdain to anticipate that hour out of reverence for His Mother . . . In the water changed into the wine of healing and strengthening could they not see a figure of John's baptism transformed into baptism by the Spirit?" *(The Gospel of Jesus Christ,* vol. 1, Westminster, Md., 1938).

Fifteen hundred years ago, St. Gaudentius, consecrated bishop of Brescia by St. Ambrose (d. about 400), wrote that at Cana Mary asked for wine in the name of the Church. He preached on the Easter and Pentecostal significance of the wedding feast of Cana, seeing in the third day of the wedding the anticipation of the third day of the resurrection, and in the wine supplied for the wedding by the Savior the foretaste of the wine of the Spirit poured at Pentecost. P.-L. Carle writing in a European magazine said, "Realizing that her Son is embarking upon a new life (John 2, 4), Mary's request for help is totally subordinated to his will (John 2, 3, 5). Her prayer is more perfect than the prayers of Martha and Mary (John 11, 21, 32), more perfect than the petitions of those who repeated and urged their requests, e.g., the

Roman official at Cana (John 4, 46-54) and the Canaanite woman with the possessed daughter (Matthew 15, 21-28)." Fr. R. E. Brown of the United States commented, "Our Lady's faith obtained the miracle of Cana which led the followers of Jesus to believe in him."

The final mention of the Mary of history in the New Testament is in the Acts, a strangely neglected text in view of its catechetical and ecumenical importance. In 1973 Rene Laurentin gave a lecture on Mary in the Communion of Saints to the international conference held at Birmingham, England, sponsored by the Ecumenical Society of the Blessed Virgin Mary. He noted that not since 1950 had any study worth noting appeared on the verse of Acts, "All these with one accord devoted themselves to prayer, together with the women and Mary, the mother of Jesus, and with his brothers" (New Oxford Annotated, 1, 14). In 1950 Cardinal Bea gave a paper on the subject at a congress in Rome, and, as it happened, later in 1973, after Laurentin's conference in England, Benedetto Prete, an Italian Dominican, published a long article on the same verse, on which the following paragraphs depend.

The reference in the Acts is evidence of the influence of Mary's presence in the apostolic Church. The place is the upper room in Jerusalem. The time is the waiting period between the final appearance and disappearance of the Risen Jesus forty days after the resurrection as described at the very beginning of Acts and the day of Pentecost. The Virgin Mary is part of the core group of the infant Church. On Pentecost they will be "filled with the Holy Spirit and begin to speak foreign tongues as the Spirit" gives "them the gift of speech" (2, 4). The Mother of Jesus is among her Son's followers who "remained faithful to the teaching of the apostles, to the brotherhood, to the breaking of bread, and to the prayers" (2, 42).

By several precise words St. Luke stresses the sense of

community in the group to which Mary belonged: they
were praying "with one accord," in harmony, in cordial
agreement, believers united heart and soul (4, 32). The
phrase, "with one accord" (the same Latin root as the word
"cordial") recalls the advice of Deuteronomy to love God
with one's whole heart and one's whole soul, and the response of the people at Sinai in Exodus 19, "Everything the
Lord has said we will do."

The Acts call Mary "Mother of Jesus," that is, mother of
the same Jesus who has been taken up to heaven to the
Father's right hand, the same Jesus who has appeared to his
followers over the forty-day period, the same Jesus who
promised to send his friends the gift of his Holy Spirit.
St. Luke focuses on the fullness of Jesus, and his reference
to the Mother of Jesus is at the service of his emphasis on
Christ. In the opening two chapters of St. Luke's gospel
and in St. John's accounts of Cana and Calvary the titles
of the Virgin Mary reflect the Church's faith in Jesus, the
son of Mary. Thus she is "Mother of my Lord" in
Elizabeth's greeting (Luke 1, 43), that is, "mother of the
messianic king"; she is "woman" in St. John's gospel, evoca-
tive of the first woman, for she is the new Eve, and the
symbol of the Church, the Jerusalem from above, the new
Israel, the "woman" of the New Testament, as God's people
of the old covenant were represented under woman figures,
daughter of Sion, spouse of God. In calling Mary "Mother
of Jesus" the Acts are thinking of the Son of Mary who was
raised up for our justification, whose Spirit brings power to
his Church.

The likenesses between the opening of St. Luke's gospel
and the beginning of the Acts of the Apostles are deliberate.
"We see Mary prayerfully imploring the gift of the Spirit who
had already overshadowed her in the Annunciation" (constitution on the Church, n 59). At the annunciation Mary
awaits the overshadowing Spirit; guided by the Spirit, she

hastens to her cousin, bringing the good news to the household of Zachary, answering Elizabeth's greeting with her song of joy and thanksgiving, the Magnificat. In the upper room Mary again awaits the Spirit, this time under the leadership of the apostles, although artists can easily be forgiven for putting her at the center of the apostolic band, as the eucharistic prayer of remembrance does and the rosary does. Now she awaits the outpouring of the Spirit so that Jesus may be born at Pentecost in his brothers and sisters, members of the Church. The explosion of charismatic joy carries through the Book of the Acts, e.g., when the word is brought to Samaria and received with great rejoicing (Acts 8).

Blessed Virgin Mary,
Model of the Church in the Liturgy

THE SENSE of Mary as model of the Church is closely allied to enriched biblical understanding of the Mother of Jesus. This way of speaking of the Blessed Virgin may sound strange to some Catholics, even cold in comparison with many beloved popular titles of our Lady. Yet the Mary-Church relationship is among the earliest Christian themes. When the Assumption was defined as dogma by Pius XII in 1950 Catholic thinkers, especially those engaged in dialogue with members of other Christian Churches, were led to ponder more deeply the intimate bond between Mary and the Church.

With a word of warning about the danger of attempting to condense complex developments in a single word or single phrase, we can say that the consideration of our Lady in Catholic theology and devotion has moved in the last thirty years from a "privilege" stress to a "community" emphasis. Without denying to the Blessed Virgin the uniqueness of the great things God has done for her, e.g., the privileged character of her preservation from original sin and her anticipated full union, body and soul, with the victorious Christ, her Son, we have become more sensitive to the larger Church dimension, the ecclesial import, of the Mother of Jesus in both doctrine and devotion.

In his letter on the promotion of devotion to Mary, *Marialis cultus,* which centers on the revised liturgy, Pope Paul called attention to the "theme of Mary and the Church, which has been inserted into the Missal texts in a variety of aspects, matching the many and varied relations existing between the Mother of Jesus and the Church." (no. 11). The Immaculate Conception conveys the beginning of the Church, spotless bride of Christ; the Assumption is the image of what must still come to pass for the whole Church, as the Council said, "The Mother of Jesus, already glorified body and soul in heaven, is the image and the beginning of the Church as it is to be perfected in the world to come and here on earth. Until the day of the Lord arrives (2 Peter 3, 10), she shines out as sign of sure hope and comfort for the wayfaring people of God" (Constitution on the Church, no. 68).

The American bishops wrote in their joint pastoral, "What the Church has said about the effects of redemption in Mary, she has affirmed in other ways and at other times of us all. The Immaculate Conception and the Assumption . . . are basically affirmations about the nature of human salvation" (no. 111). We see Mary not simply as privileged exception to the general pattern, but as the first instance of the saving plan of the Father of mercies for all who belong to Christ. First in faith, the Virgin Mary was the first to receive the fruits of redemption in Christ.

What does it mean to call Mary "type of the Church," or "archetype of the Church"? Consider the meaning of the word "symbol." We are used to arbitrary symbols, e.g., by agreement red and green lights are accepted as stop-and-go signals. In art certain symbols are used for saints: a lily for St. Joseph, a lion for St. Jerome. Advertisers spend fortunes to impress on the public memory their distinctive "logos," e.g., golden arches for hamburger, a racing dog for a bus company. By "symbol" we usually mean today something different from what is signified; in fact we often say, "It is only a symbol." But in its original meaning "symbol" meant in some way the very reality signified, a first realization of the object to which it pointed, as in the sacraments, which are not only signs of the realities of grace but actually effect union with Christ. When we call Mary "type or symbol or archetype" of the Church, we regard her not as an arbitrary figure of the Church, but as the living and perfect exemplar of the Church, of what it means to be a member of Christ. The choice of Mary as type of the Church is not a mere human convention; she was chosen by God to be perfect model of the Church of which she is herself a member, first of the followers of Jesus.

In Mary the Church has already begun to exist. It is "part of Mary's vocation that she should prefigure the Church, living in the individual mode the mysteries which the Church would live in the community mode" (N. D. O'Donoghue, O.C.D.). In the liturgy constitution (1963), Mary is called "the most excellent fruit of the redemption, spotless model of the Church" (no.103). The constitution on the Church (1964) said, "In the Blessed Virgin the Church has already achieved a perfection whereby she exists without stain or wrinkle (Eph. 5, 27)" (no. 65).

The Virgin Mary never stands alone; any doctrine about her has to be basically about her Son and his saving work. Freedom from original sin is not so much Mary's privilege as it is a necessity for her role in salvation. His Mother's influence on the upbringing of the boy Jesus was so important that in God's special providence she was put beyond the reach of original sin. The Father chose her to sum up the expectation of the Chosen People, to be the immaculate mother of the Redeemer. As the Council Fathers said, Mary was graced in her origins that she might give herself wholeheartedly to the saving work of her Son.

The "be it done unto me" needed to be spoken by one who was supremely holy, with all the freedom of one whose choices were unclouded by original and personal sin (as expressed by E. Yarnold, S.J.). In continuity with Israel of old, Christianity began not with a biological affirmation but with Mary's act of faith in God's intervention. Along with St. Elizabeth and St. Luke the Church hails Mary as the blessed one who has believed, and therefore the Lord's promises to her will be fulfilled.

The oldest Christian reflection on Mary after the New Testament was that she was "new Eve" as early as the mid-second century. The first Eve put her faith in the deceitful word of Satan, the new Eve was faithful to God's promise through Gabriel. In 1866 John Henry Newman, famous Anglican convert to Catholicism, appealed to early references to Mary as "new Eve" in support of the Immaculate Conception, defined as dogma in 1854. He wrote that "new Eve" was "the great rudimental teaching of antiquity from its earliest date concerning her . . . the aspect under which she comes to us, in the writings of the Fathers." Even before the 1854 definition, Newman had written in his *Meditations and Devotions* (published after his death): "Though, as St. Austin says, we do not like to name her in the same breath with mention of sin, yet, certainly she would have been a frail being, like Eve, without the grace of God. A more abundant gift of grace made her what she was from the first . . . There is no difference in kind between her and us, though an inconceivable difference of degree. She and we are both simply saved by the grace of Christ . . . can we refuse to see that, according to these Fathers, who are earliest of the early, Mary was a *typical woman* like Eve, that both were endowed with special gifts of grace, and that Mary succeeded where Eve failed?"

There is no clear biblical evidence for the Immaculate Conception, a doctrine that gradually took shape in the consciousness of the Church, first in the belief of the faithful, finally in the papal proclamation by Pius IX in 1854. Newman says in his *Apologia* that the dogma was not believed by the faithful because proclaimed by the Pope, but proclaimed because believed. That does not mean that the official acts of popes and bishops merely sanction what the "referendum" has already determined, giving force of law to the opinion of the faithful, for the magisterium protects the Christian faith lest it dissipate into a welter of conflicting positions.

Notwithstanding the lack of definitive biblical backing for the Immaculate Conception, a German Franciscan B. Langemeyer has suggested a possible biblical basis on the grounds there is continuity as well as discontinuity between the old covenant and the new. A ready example is the comparison by contrast between Adam and Jesus Christ as "new Adam." We who have been modelled on the earthly man are to be modelled in the future on the heavenly man (1 Cor. 15, 49). As St. Paul put it to the Romans, the first Adam prefigured the Adam to come, but the gift considerably outweighed the fall (5, 16), Jesus is the final Adam, whose obedience healed the disobedience of the ancient Adam. In commemorating Mary's free obedience, "Behold the handmaid of the Lord, be it done unto me according to your word," the Council continued by recalling her early title of "new Eve" (no. 56).

How does Mary fit into the "continuity and discontinuity" between the Testaments?

There is a follow-through between Hebrew past and Christian present, for if the first testament had led only to sin, there would have been no "holy remnant" that survived. Then the Gospel would have been an altogether fresh beginning, not the fulfillment of the promises. By her consent in faith Mary is the culmination of the faithful remnant of Israel. The Scriptures show us a line of great

men as "standard-bearers" of redemption: Adam, Abraham,
Moses and others; the bible gives us also a parallel line of
believers in the saving actions of the Lord, the great women,
Eve, Sara, Miriam, even the whole people of God under
feminine images, as "bride of God," "daughter of Sion."

The Bible is filled with praise of Abraham who followed
the unknown God in faith into an alien land and became
the ancestor of the Messiah, through his son Isaac and
grandson Jacob who was renamed Israel. The epistle to the
Hebrews (11, 11) recalls that Sara too, wife of Abraham,
was made able to conceive Isaac because she believed that
God was faithful to his promises. In Mary's response, "Let
it be as you say," the covenant expectation reached perfect
expression. The initial holiness of Mary's Immaculate Conception shows not only the discontinuity of special privilege, the divine break-through, the surprise of the Incarnation, but also the continuity of God's merciful dealings with
his people, preparing for the sending of the Messiah as the
"Son of man," born of the Virgin Mary.

St. Ambrose (d. 397) called Mary "type of the Church."
According to him Mary shows forth in herself the figure
of the holy Church, and he applied Old Testament texts to
her, "How beautiful are those things which have been prophesied of Mary under the figure of the Church." The
Council followed St. Ambrose in explaining the relationship
between Mary and the Church, "The Mother of God is a
type of the Church, in the order of faith, charity and perfect
union with Christ" *(Lumen gentium,* no. 63). "By the power
of the Holy Spirit, the Church imitates the mother of her
Lord, and, like a virgin, maintains undiminished faith, steadfast hope, and sincere charity" (no. 63).

The liturgy decree called Mary "the most excellent
fruit of the redemption, the spotless model" in whom the
Church sees its own ideal (no. 103). Mary Immaculate is a
sign of the love of Christ for his bride the Church: he

cleanses her in the bath of his own blood to make her all-holy and free from every stain of sin. What God did for the Mother of his Son, enriching her with his grace from the first instant of her existence, in anticipation of the merits of Christ the Redeemer, is the sign of his saving intent towards all human beings.

When Mary answered, "Let it be done unto me according to your word," the Word was made flesh and dwelt amongst us. One of the earliest authors to describe Mary as "new Eve" was St. Irenaeus (d. ab. 200). He wrote of Mary by her obedience helping untie the knot of disobedience tied by the first Eve. He also commented on Mary's Magnificat, "Mary rejoiced, and speaking prophetically in the Church's name said, 'My Soul magnifies the Lord.' " Pope Paul incorporated the thought of St. Irenaeus into *Marialis cultus:*

"Mary is the Virgin in prayer . . . her pre-eminent prayer is her Magnificat, the song of messianic times which joins the joy of the ancient and the new Israel. As St. Irenaeus seems to suggest, in Mary's canticle the rejoicing of Abraham, who foresaw the Messiah, was heard once more (John 8, 56), and the voice of the Church rang out in prophetic anticipation: 'In her exultation Mary prophetically declared in the name of the Church: "My soul magnifies the Lord . . . " ' " (no. 19). Mary's hymn has become part of the official evening prayer of the Church. As Paul Claudel, French poet and diplomat, wrote to a friend (Sept. 25, 1907), "The Magnificat was not said once for all in the garden at Hebron; it was put in the mouth of the Church for all the centuries."

In the new Sacramentary the second common preface of our Lady is described, "The Church praises God in the words of Mary," and the preface reads in part, "In celebrating the memory of the Virgin Mary it is our great joy to glorify your love for us in the words of her song of thanksgiving. What wonders you have worked throughout the world. All generations share your boundless love."

The present revised liturgy presents Mary Immaculate as the great model of holy Church. The feast of the Immaculate Conception, December 8, has been kept as the patronal feast of the Catholic Church in the United States since 1847. The new preface in the Sacramentary is filled with the conviction that what God did for the mother of his Son is the sign of his mercy towards all members of holy Church. The preface begins, "Father, all-powerful and ever-living God, we do well always and everywhere to give you thanks. You allowed no stain of Adam's sin to touch the Virgin Mary. Full of grace, she was to be a worthy mother of your Son, your sign of favor to the Church at its beginning, and the promise of its perfection as the bride of Christ, radiant in its beauty."

The Council, and subsequent developments, again especially in the liturgy, have brought out the significance of our Lady's Assumption for the self-understanding of the Church. Earlier in the 20th century there was a re-discovery of the Church as "mystical body" of Christ. Great theologians like the Belgian Emile Mersch, S.J. (d. 1940) studied St. Paul's imagery for the Church, with Christ as the head, and those who belong to the Church as the members, like members of a human body controlled by the head. This led to the encyclical on the Mystical Body of Christ by Pius XII in 1943, which had an important appendix on Mary, mother of Christ the head and the spiritual mother of the members of the mystical body of Christ.

At the Second Vatican Council another biblical insight about the Church came to the fore, the Church as "people of God," a people on pilgrimage. No single image, however, exhausts the mystery of the Church. Through the Mother of Jesus the Council conveyed further aspects of the Church, for example, the Church is also "bride of Christ," an important truth with deep roots in tradition and scripture. The Assumption brings out the understanding of the Church as bride of Christ. Faithful to his promise, the Bridegroom, the Risen Jesus, has gone to prepare a place for his bride the Church. In the doctrine of Mary's Assumption, oldest explicit feast of Mary in the calendar, we celebrate the nuptials between Christ and his Church.

Mary, Mother of Jesus, is also "daughter of the Church." In Mary, joined to Christ in glory in the fulness of her person body and soul, the pilgrim Church sees the successful completion of its own journey. In the strength of her Son's exaltation, Mary has joined him in heaven, representing the Church of which she is herself a member. The Resurrection remains the central Christian mystery; the Assumption of Mary is the living sign of the Church's call to glory, to union with the triumphant Jesus, to perfect, victorious redemption.

There are encouraging ecumenical possibilities in seeing Mary as model of the Church, bride of Christ. One ancient approach was to apply Psalm 44 (45) to both Mary and the Church in liturgical prayer, as is still done today. The psalm is a song for the marriage of the king, and begins with the words, "My heart overflows with noble words. To the king I must speak the song I have made; my tongue as nimble as the pen of a scribe." It contains the familiar verse, "On your right hand stands the queen in gold of Ophir . . ." Jaroslav Pelikan, the Lutheran historian of doctrine, urges Christians to take seriously the Marian and ecclesial implications of Ps. 44 (45), in an article in *The Christian Century* (January 6, 1965) "How I Am Making Up My Mind: Tradition, Reformation and Development." (This essay was reprinted in the book, *Frontline Theology,* ed. by D. Peerman, Richmond, Va., 1967). Pelikan wrote of the role of liturgy in the history of doctrine, an awareness deepened for him by Orthodox and Catholic contacts; by way of example, he wrote, "the history of the exegesis of the 45th psalm reveals both a fascinating segment of the development of devotion to Mary and a continuity of concern for the nature of the Church in relation to Israel as seen in the typology of the king's daughter in that Psalm."

Serge Boulgakov, famous Russian emigré theologian who died in 1944, and a selection of whose writings has just been published, including an essay on our Lady, "The Burning Bush," commented also on Mary as model of the Church in the classical interpretation of Ps. 44 (45) in Christian antiquity, the queen standing at the right hand of the king. Dr. Ross Mackenzie, representing Presbyterian thought, has written that the symbol "bride" belongs preeminently in the eschatological perspective, looking to future fulfillment, for the Church as bride is before all the heavenly Church. He writes, "Mary is a sign of contradiction, precisely as the one who bears witness to a future that is of God's making and not ours."

In the current liturgy of the hours, official daily prayer of the Church, the prayer that follows Ps. 44 (45) on Monday evening of the second week, reads as follows: "When you took on flesh, Lord Jesus, you made a marriage of mankind with God. Help us to be faithful to your word and endure our exile bravely, until we are called to your heavenly marriage feast to which the Virgin Mary, exemplar of your Church, has preceded us."

While the Council was still in progress, Archbishop Philip Pocock of Toronto, sent his people a letter for the month of May, 1964, "Mary in the Mystery of the Church," a portion of which was used by the bishops of the United States in their joint pastoral, *Behold Your Mother, Woman of Faith*. The Canadian archbishop related the Assumption of Mary to the Risen Christ and the entire Church: "The Blessed Virgin experiences already now, in the fullest sense, that Christ is the 'resurrection and the life' (John 11, 25), and that he who is in Jesus 'is not under the judgment but has passed from death to life' (John 5, 24). This is what we mean when we confess the assumption of our Lady into heaven. She is now with her divine son, clothed in her body made imperishable, constantly reminding the Church that Jesus does not want to be alone, but always face to face with another in love. Our Lady, sharing in the glory of her Son, strengthens our hope in the destiny of the entire Church. This was the vision of St. John when, contemplating the age to come, he saw the holy city, new Jerusalem, coming down out of heaven from God, made ready, as a bride adorned for her husband (Apoc. 21, 2)." (in *Behold Your Mother,* no. 61).

The bond between Mary assumed into heaven and the glorious destiny of the entire Church is stated in the new proper preface for the feast of the Assumption, August 15, "Lady Day in Harvest" as it was once called in England. The Church is addressing the Father, "Today the Virgin Mother of God was taken up into heaven to be the beginning and the pattern of the Church in its perfection, and a sign of sure hope and comfort for your pilgrim people. You would not allow decay to touch her body, for she had given birth in the glory of the Incarnation to your Son, the Lord of all life" (see also *Lumen gentium,* no. 68).

The Blessed Virgin and Ecumenism

SINCE the Protestant Reformation in the sixteenth century the Virgin Mary has been a sign of contradiction among Western Christians. Along with the papacy, Catholic devotion to the Mother of Jesus has been a special difficulty to Protestants, although Christians are at last facing these differences openly and charitably. A good illustration is the recent agreed statement of the international Anglican and Roman Catholic Commission, from the Venice meeting of September, 1976, on "authority in the Church." After noting that the Roman Catholic doctrine of infallibility is subject to conditions which "preclude the idea that the Pope is an inspired oracle communicating fresh revelation, or that he can speak independently of his fellow bishops and the church, or on matters not concerning faith or morals," the Venice statement continues, "For the Roman Catholic Church, the Pope's dogmatic definitions, which, fulfilling the criteria of infallibility, are preserved from error, do no more but no less than express the mind of the church on issues concerning the divine revelation. Even so, special difficulties are created by the recent Marian dogmas, because Anglicans doubt the appropriateness, or even the possibility, of defining them as essential to the faith of believers."

In 1962 Brother Max Thurian of the French Calvinist monastic community of Taizé wrote *Mary Mother of the Lord, Figure of the Church* (Faith Press, London, 1963; the American edition by Herder and Herder, New York 1964, which has gone out of print, was titled, *Mary, Mother of All Christians).* Thurian laments that divided Christendom today resembles the soldiers dividing the garments of Christ on Calvary, in painful contrast to the unity of Mary and the beloved disciple. All the same he is confident that the Blessed Virgin "by her faith, her hope, her charity, and her prayers will be a spiritual mother in Mother Church, of which she is the living and humble representative."

What is the place of the Virgin Mary in the more open ecumenical climate of recent years? These reflections on Mary and Christian unity are in four parts. The first takes up current developments; the second gives three difficulties and three signs of hope; the third considers two outstanding examples of thought on the Virgin Mary by Christians of non-Roman Catholic traditions, John C. de Satgé of England and J. A. Ross Mackenzie of the United States; part four will be about the Ecumenical Society of the Blessed Virgin Mary.

RECENT DEVELOPMENTS

The consideration of the Blessed Virgin is not yet a major concern in ecumenical dialogue, although there is a clear recognition this topic must be finally faced. On the Catholic side the Second Vatican Council showed a keen awareness of the difficulties other Christians find in Catholic doctrine and devotion about the Mother of Jesus. There were some note-worthy efforts prior to the Council, e.g., in 1950 Père Paul Couturier (d. 1953) of France edited the book, *Dialogue on the Virgin,* with contributions from many sources, including a meditation on Mary by the eldest daughter of the Booths, founders of the Salvation Army.

Couturier was encouraged by the then Cardinal Montini in his ecumenical efforts, through Cardinal Gerlier of Lyons. Couturier's simple prayer for unity became famous, "May the visible unity of the kingdom of God come as Christ wills and by the means he wills." For the week of universal prayer in 1952 he wrote another prayer that includes these words: "When the attitude of Christians is that of Mary, when the Virgin's reply echoes silently in the hearts of us all, this vast silent prayer, guided and led by the voice of the Virgin, will break like a wave before the throne of God in an irresistible supplication. And once again there will be unity, 'by the action of the Holy Spirit.' How could she who on earth said to her Son: 'They have no more wine,' not say to him in heaven: 'They no longer have unity'? And seeing that she stood at the foot of the cross, her heart at one with that of him who was crucified, in heaven she must stand at the feet of the Lamb, her heart at one with the Lamb's in his supplication to his Father for the unity of the whole Christian family: 'Father, let them be one, as we are one.' Let all Christians join her and listen to her as she stands at the foot of the cross and at the feet of the Lamb" (from M. Villain, S.M., *Unity: A History and Some Reflections,* London, 1963).

On November 21, 1963, the Council published two documents: the dogmatic constitution on the Church, *Lumen gentium* ("Light to the nations") with its concluding chapter, "The Blessed Virgin Mary, Mother of God, in the Mystery of Christ and the Church," and the decree on ecumenism with its confident title, "The re-establishment of unity" *(Redintegratio unitatis).* The Church document urged Catholics to avoid speaking about Mary in ways that cause undue difficulty to other Christians; the Council's own tone is strongly scriptural and patristic. Moreover, the chapter on Mary used with great restraint such words as "mediatrix," which along with possible pastoral and catechetical problems cause grave difficulties for Protestants. The decree on ecumenism pleaded for unity, while acknowledging the present sad reality that we Christians are "separated brethren." The final remedy for our disunity is faith in Christ.

The ecumenical document stated that "when comparing one doctrine with another, we should remember that there exists an order or hierarchy of truths within Catholic doctrine, since the truths vary in their relationship to the foundation of the Christian faith" (no. 11). The decree used Mary as an example of "order or hierarchy of truths" in paragraph 20, which began with a biblical formula very close to the profession of faith from the World Council of Churches meeting at New Delhi, 1961: "Our thoughts turn first to those Christians who make open confession of Jesus Christ as God and Lord, and as the sole Mediator between God and men, to the glory of the one God, Father, Son and Holy Spirit. We are indeed aware that there exist considerable divergencies from the doctrine of the Catholic Church concerning Christ himself, the Word of God made flesh, the work of Redemption, and consequently concerning the mystery and ministry of the Church, and the role of Mary in the plan of salvation."

Differences among Christians about Mary's role in the plan of salvation go back to differences about "the mystery and ministry of the Church," and even more radically back to doctrinal differences concerning the Word made flesh and the work of Redemption. Our Lady is intimately joined to both Christ and the Church. The order or hierachy of truths can be compared to a series of concentric circles with Christ as the center; other truths are measured according to their proximity to him, the heart of our faith. As the Council stated, the role of Mary in God's saving plan is rooted in Christ and bound up with the body of Christ which is his Church. The first conciliar document, on the liturgy, 1963, said that Mary is "inseparably joined to the saving work of Christ, the spotless model of the Church" which looks to her always as model and helper (no. 103).

Anglican interest in our Lady goes back to pre-Reformation roots. The "Caroline divines" of the seventeenth century made a place for the Virgin Mary in their theology and piety. In this century the Fellowship of St. Alban and St. Sergius has promoted exchanges between Anglicans and Eastern Christians, and published sets of essays on our Lady, as by Dr. E. L. Mascall and the late Orthodox expert, V. Lossky (d. 1958).

In the major Churches of the Reform, Lutheranism and Calvinism (including Presbyterianism) there have been only a few efforts in this area, but what has been done is solid and promising. On the international scene a Russian Orthodox priest, Serge Boulgakov, introduced the role of Mary in the communion of saints in an address to the first meeting of the Faith and Order Conference in 1927, at Lausanne, Switzerland. "Faith and Order" is the branch of the World Council of Churches concerned with doctrinal and liturgical issues. Boulgakov was reminded that the topic was not on the agenda, but insisted that the Theotokos, the God-bearer, the Mother of God, is an indispensable element in Orthodox understanding of the Church. A bit more attention was given to the Marian theme in the subsequent meetings of Faith and Order in 1938 and 1952, but little more has happened in the World Council of Churches since then. Yet Lukas Vischer, the secretary of Faith and Order, gave a remarkable conference at Princeton University, New Jersey, in the spring of 1971 on Mary, type of the Church and type of mankind.

There is a possibility that when and if the Catholic Church becomes a full member of the World Council of Churches,

Eastern Christians not in union with Rome, particularly the great world of Greek and Russian Orthodoxy, may play a reconciling role between divided Churches of the West with respect to the all-holy Virgin Mother of God who is so prominent in Eastern life and worship, living icon of God's grace.

The Lutheran-Roman Catholic consultations have been going on over a decade in the United States; they are now working on a consensus statement on papal infallibility. For the meeting of September, 1975, at Lutheran request, a paper was assigned on the definitions of the Immaculate Conception and the Assumption as instances of the exercise of papal infallibility. It was my privilege to be invited to give that paper; the experience of the meeting was pleasant and interesting, but I came away convinced that a better ecumenical introduction to the Mother of Jesus would be to stake out possible common ground first and only then take up the peculiarly difficult doctrines of Mary's freedom from original sin and her Assumption to full union with the Risen Christ, with the further complication of the papal definitions of these doctrines in 1854 and 1950. Both the Immaculate Conception and the Assumption are bound to seem arbitrary unless one is first convinced of Mary's place in God's merciful plan of salvation and her abiding union with her glorified Son in the communion of saints.

The document from the Secretariat for Promoting Christian Unity, dated August 15, 1970, makes the same suggestion under the rubric of the "hierarchy of truths." "Certainly all revealed truths demand the same acceptance of faith, but according to the greater or lesser proximity that they have to the basis of the revealed mystery, they are variously placed with regard to one another and have varying connections among themselves. For example, the dogma of Mary's Immaculate Conception, which may not be isolated from what the Council of Ephesus declares about Mary, the Mother of God, presupposes, before it can be properly grasped in a true life of faith, the dogma of grace to which it is linked and which in its turn necessarily rests upon the redemptive incarnation of the Word."

THREE DIFFICULTIES AND THREE HOPEFUL SIGNS

The first trouble-spot is the relationship between Scripture, tradition and the Church's teaching authority. Protestants find unbiblical, even anti-biblical, Catholic insistence there are revealed truths about the Virgin Mary not clearly contained in Scripture. The recent Council did not speak of tradition as a source of revelation separate from the Scriptures, and many reputable Catholic scholars hold all revealed doctrines are contained in sacred scripture. The Holy Spirit guides the Church, both the bishops who teach and the people who believe and celebrate, to ever fuller appreciation of truths hidden in the Bible.

A second basic difference is Mary as a symbol of human beings corresponding with grace and thereby meriting salvation. In the classical Protestant outlook on justification the Catholic view of the Virgin Mary gravely endangers the all-sufficient saving work of God himself. This was the protest made by the Swiss Calvinist, Karl Barth (d. 1968) who defended so strongly the divinity of Jesus and the virginal conception. The Second Vatican Council called Mary the perfect figure of the Church. Protestants object that Mary is being taken as model of the Catholic Church, the Church of Rome. It is charged that the historical Mary, a humble obedient woman, has been changed into a symbol of the Church cooperating with prevenient grace in order to merit salvation, and that this is an erroneous understanding of the Church.

The third difficulty is the most obvious, because it touches common practice as well as belief: Catholic devotion to Mary. From the beginning of the Reformation Protestants were forbidden to call upon the saints, even Saint Mary, in prayer. The precise word for this is "invocation," asking our Lady and the saints to "pray for us," to "intercede" on our behalf with Christ the supreme Intercessor. The reasons for forbidding invocation of the saints were: a) a reaction to pre-Reformation abuses in the cult of the saints, b) fear that any calling upon the saints meant diminished confidence in Jesus the one Mediator. In forbidding recourse in prayer to Mary and the saints the Reform broke with a practice reaching back to early centuries and found in the universal Church; it persists in the entire Christian East to the present day.

SIGNS OF HOPE

There are many signs of hope for ecumenical agreement on Mary; we take up three. The first is the common study of the scriptures, with scholars finding new depths of meaning about Mary in the Gospels. Not only is Mary mother of Jesus the Savior, for St. Luke and St. John she is also the ideal model of the Church. In the nativity chapters of St. Luke Mary is the "daughter of Sion." summarizing the long expectations of Israel, anticipating the new Israel, the Christian Church. For St. John the Mother of Jesus is called "woman" at Cana and on Calvary, with a possible link to "the woman clothed with the sun" of the twelfth chapter of the Book of Revelation. The compassionate concern of Mary at Cana and her sorrowing presence at the cross were intensely personal facets of her life, but St. John sees her as larger than a private person. She is the model believer, the figure of the Church called to faith, the "woman" par excellence, showing faith even before the first of her Son's signs at Cana and faithfully standing by the cross of Jesus as the representative of Mother Church.

Due to appear in the fall of 1978, with the Catholic Paulist Press of New York and the Lutheran Fortress Press of Philadelphia as co-publishers, is the book *Mary in the New Testament. A Collaborative Assessment by Protestant, Anglican and Roman Catholic Scholars.* The editors are Raymond E. Brown and Joseph A. Fitzmyer, Catholics, and the Lutherans Karl P. Donfried and John Reumann. The book is based on discussions by a dozen scholars, e.g., Catholic, Lutheran, Anglican, and Presbyterian. The same research group produced the book *Peter in the New Testament,* in 1973, also an outgrowth of the Lutheran-Roman Catholic consultations. The book on Mary records substantial agreement on how Christians of the first two centuries pictured Mary.

The second international ecumenical conference organized by the Ecumenical Society of the Blessed Virgin Mary was held in 1973 at Birmingham, England, on the theme, "Mary in the Bible." Co-presidents were Anglican Bishop Cyril K. Sansbury, then the general secretary of the British Council of Churches, and Bishop Alan C. Clark, of the Roman Catholic Ecumenical Commission, who has since become ordinary of the new see of East Anglia. In his opening remarks Bishop Clark said, "Wherever Mary is to be found today and wherever she is found in our respective traditions, one thing is certain: she is there in the Bible. The problem is how to reconcile the freedom of her biblical simplicity with the undoubted theological depths she inspires . . . We cannot afford the luxury and comfort of an unreflected faith if we take seriously our ecumenical comitment. Before the extremes of retreat into a barricaded fundamental fortress and radical criticism that is reductionist and nothing more, our separate wisdom has been found

devastatingly wanting . . . We are united in our acceptance
of the Gospel, and in that Good News we find Mary" (from
notes taken at the talk).

A second promising area is the study of early Christian
authors particularly at the beginning of the patristic period.
As early as the second century Mary is described as "new
Eve," in contrast to the disobedient original Eve, e.g., in St.
Justin, mid-2nd Century, and more fully in St. Irenaeus (d.
about 200). By St. Jerome's time (d. 420) it was axiomatic
to say, as the Second Vatican Council recalled (no. 56),
"Death through Eve, life through Mary."

The American Lutheran expert on early Christian authors,
Dr. Jaroslav Pelikan, has often written on Mary, e.g., the
article in the *Encyclopedia Brittanica* (vol. 14). In a study
on St. Athanasius, bishop of Alexandria, who defended the
faith of Nicea in the divinity of Christ in the fourth century,
Dr. Pelikan wrote of St. Athanasius' doctrine and devotion
on Mary. The bishop proposed Mary as model particularly
to virgins; Dr. Pelikan suggests he was influenced in his piety
towards the Virgin Mary by contemporary beliefs about her,
particularly the title, Mother of God, already familiar to him
a century before it would be defined at Ephesus in 431 A.D.
(in Pelikan's book, *Development of Christian Doctrine:
Some Historical Prolegomena,* New Haven, Conn., 1969).

A third encouraging factor is the revived interest in the
writings on Mary of the great Reformers. An American
publisher (Augsburg of Minneapolis) brought out for the
450th anniversary of the beginning of Luther's Reform,
1467-1967, a paperback edition of Luther's *Commentary on
the Magnificat,* written 1520/1521. As a sample, Luther
commented on the line, "My soul magnifies God, the Lord."
as follows, "God lets us remain poor and hapless, because
we cannot leave His tender gifts undefiled or keep an even
mind, but let our spirits rise or fall according to how He
gives or takes away His gifts. But Mary's heart remains the

same at all times; she lets God have His will with her and draws from it all only a good comfort, joy, and trust in God. Thus we too should do; that would be to sing a right Magnificat."

It might seem a return to Reformation sources would accentuate differences between Protestant and Catholics. In fact, however, the Reformers never lost their veneration for the Virgin Mary, even though they forbade calling on her in prayer. During the subsequent polemic centuries of Reformation and Counter-Reformation, positions on Mary became more rigid on both sides, so that a return to the 16th century writings holds out hope. As a Belgian Protestant, Gaston Westphal, wrote in *Life and Faith of a Protestant* (1966), in the chapter, "Contemplation at Cana," "Let us not forget . . . the book by Luther on the Magnificat, the Commentary on the Annunciation by Calvin, the belief of Zwingli in the Assumption. Let us remember also that in theory, if not in fact, the dogma of Ephesus, the Christological dogma before all others, is enshrined in all our confessions of faith, along with the dogma of the Trinity and the Chalcedonian dogma of the two natures of Christ."

RECENT PROTESTANT WRITINGS ON THE VIRGIN MARY

The first example is John C. de Satgé of England, whose book appeared in the United States in late 1976 as *Down to Earth: The New Protestant Vision of the Virgin Mary* (Consortium Books, Wilmington, N.C., cloth and paperback). It was published simultaneously in England by the Anglican firm, the Society for the Promoting of Christian Knowledge (the famous S.P.C.K.), under the title, *Mary and the Christian Gospel.* DeSatgé comes from a strong Evangelical, that is, Protestant, Anglican background, in contrast to Anglo-

Catholicism or High Church Anglicanism: his orientation
is decisively Reformed rather than inclining towards Rome.
He first got interested in the topic of Mary in 1956, when
he took part in a Lutheran-Anglican-Orthodox conference
at Lund, Sweden. His first published reflections came out
in the book edited by E.L. Mascall and H.S. Box, *The
Blessed Virgin Mary: Essays by Anglican Writers* (London,
1963), "Towards an Evangelical Re-appraisal," an essay
containing the germs of his later thought, developing out of
meditation on Romans chapter eight, God's predestining
love for man. He began by summarizing Protestant objec-
tions to Marian devotion: 1) not grounded in the Scriptures;
2) dogmatic distortion; 3) religiously dangerous; 4) a pheno-
menon best explained by comparative religion and psychology.

Even here, however, deSatgé added, Christian unity requires taking Rome and Orthodoxy more seriously. In 1961
the Russian Orthodox Church became part of the World
Council of Churches and this forced the issue out in the
open. "Whether we like it or not, we are now in a certain
relation of explicit Christian fraternity with a large number
of people whose devotion to our Lady is an integral part of
their faith." Dialogue with Roman Catholics requires new
consideration as well; hence "community, responsibility,
and penitence: these are the predispositions essential to an
evangelical re-appraisal of the deep differences that exist
over the honor due to the mother of Christ."

He then asked if Evangelicals, "those of us to whom all
Marian cultus is alien," have taken to heart the Virgin's
prophecy, "All generations shall call me blessed." Might
it be Catholics have something correct in insisting on Mary's
free consent at the Annunciation? Too little attention has
been paid the central truth of Mary's motherhood, with the
Annunciation and the birth of Jesus beginning a lasting
relationship between Mary and her Son. "Since he is still

man and became man from Mary, bone of her bone and flesh of her flesh, she is still his mother."

"Christ is the second Adam, the New Man, and we are incorporated to form part of his total Humanity. Does this mean that we are adopted into a relationship not only with him but with her from whom he took his flesh? If so, then she is not only his mother; she becomes our mother too." The last sentence of the 1963 essay read, "If evangelicals are to alter their attitude towards catholic devotion to Mary, it is from deeper contemplation of the mysteries of the Person of Christ and of our membership in him that such change will come."

De Satgé was a founding member of the Ecumenical Society of the Blessed Virgin Mary, in 1967, and gave one of the first papers for the Society, November 15, 1967, "Mary in the Church: Some Matters for Ecumenical Study." He pleaded for a return to the sources in our various Christian traditions, to get back to "straight" Mariology as distinct from polemical extremes. Christians must "search their own traditions to see how the figure of our Lord's Mother appears there in Scripture and creed." We cannot ignore our differences, and compromise formulas satisfy no one. "Above all Christians will go to the One at the center of all Christian obedience and devotion."

In that 1967 conference de Satgé kept returning to the neuralgic point of the present place of Mary in the communion of saints. The Reformers had uniformly prohibited calling on the saints in prayer, even the Mother of Jesus, in reaction to abuses and convinced such petitions showed lack of confidence in Christ the Mediator. Alluding to the Vatican Council on Mary's earthly life of faith and heavenly intercession, he commented, "Some of us would be happier if there were some discussion of the change from history ('she presented him to the Father in the temple') to what one may perhaps call meta-history ('taken up to heaven she

did not lay aside the salvific duty')." He noted also that
the Council, along with seeing the Church as a pilgrim
people, also took "serious account of the Christian dead
who, as the Church goes on, and the end is delayed, form an
ever increasing proportion of the People of God and the
Body of Christ." "The possibility of colloquy with the
Blessed Virgin is one which all Protestants find it hard to
accept. It is, to my mind, far easier to praise our Lady than
to pray to her," although "any seriously ecumenical approach
to Mariology will have to deal . . . with particular relationships between members of the Church militant and the Church
triumphant."

At the Birmingham, England, ecumenical conference,
Easter week 1973, Canon René Laurentin spoke on "Mary
in the Communion of Saints." He reviewed the history of
Mary's place in the communion of saints, and the custom of
calling on her in prayer, as practiced by Catholics and
Eastern Churches but forbidden by Churches of the Reformation. Laurentin did not spare his fellow-Catholics in his
presentation. We must always see the role of Mary in total
subordination to Christ the one Savior and to his Holy Spirit,
the great Advocate. He said, "Mary is neither an understudy
for Christ, nor a substitute for the Holy Spirit." At the end
Laurentin asked, "Why does Protestantism tend to reduce
the communion of saints to the fellowship of the living, and
seem almost allergic to fellowship with the witnesses who
lived before us — the twelve and the Blessed Virgin included?
Is it simply a reaction against the cult of the saints?. . . Has
there already been a change in this key-attitude; can it still
change in the Reformed tradition?" In the ensuing discussion John de Satgé spoke of the sense of outrage Evangelicals feel that Catholic piety to the Virgin Mary and the
saints harms the majesty of Christ. "All the same," he added,
"there is a small but discernible concern for the communion
of saints."

In *Down to Earth,* his full-scale book, de Satge seeks "to find an attitude towards the Lord's mother which will include the essentials of Catholic teaching and at the same time do justice to the central impulses of evangelical Christianity." Christ is the center from which his Mother must be understood. Jesus who suffered and died is the Christ who has been raised from the dead, he is now present as guide and Lord through the power of his Holy Spirit. The evangelical recognizes Jesus as Lord and Savior in an intensely personal way, not a sentimental experience but faith in the atoning death of Jesus Christ. What bearing has this on the Virgin Mary? De Satgé's answer is, "The mystery of Jesus is that he is both brother and other. Which means that his mother was the mother of one who was both brother and other: and it is to her that we now turn to see what light the study of her may throw upon the mysteries of her Son."

De Satgé writes for the ordinary educated reader, not for scholars and specialists, in clear and beautiful English. His book may prove even more helpful to Catholics than Protestants, towards understanding the legitimacy of Mary's place in the communion of saints, why we pray to her in the liturgy and other public and private devotions. The Epistle to the Hebrews (chap. 12) mentions the "cloud of witnesses" who watch over us as we run the race of faith. De Satge feels Protestants have often overlooked the biblical bond between Old Testament and New, and thereby missed "the encouragement of heavenly supporters." At the cost of what he calls his own "emotional revolution," he dares to advocate "on Evangelical grounds the cultivation of personal relationships 'in Christ' with the blessed Virgin and all the saints . . . We should regard Mary not merely with historical interest, but with profound gratitude."

What of the recent Marian dogmas, the Immaculate Conception and the Assumption? Even here de Satgé finds grounds for ecumenical hope, so long as both beliefs be considered "under the theological control of the great evangelical certainties of the faith." In St. Paul's terms, the Assumption means Mary's predestination has achieved full conformity with the Son of God who is also her Son; she is "the splendid trophy of the Gospel's grace and power." The Christian East and the Roman West have retained what Western Protestantism has lost, the conviction that "Mary has got there."

De Satgé's book was already at the printer when he presented a paper to the Ecumenical Society at a meeting in London, February 10, 1976, at the Anglican Church of St. Marylebone. He chose as title for the conference, "The Evangelical Mary," "to refer to the effect which a new devotion to her has had upon the Christian outlook of one evangelical." "For its own good, evangelical Christianity needs a far more positive relationship with our Lord's mother and with all the saints than it has normally encouraged . . . a proper relationship with our Lord's mother safeguards the conditions essential for evangelical religion, the first of which is to know Christ as your Savior." Proper Marian devotion in its best Catholic practice and authentic Evangelical religion both come from the same fundamentals of traditional Christian theology; they stand together in defense of Christian faith.

It is encouraging to note the warm reviews de Satgé's book is receiving on both sides of the Atlantic, e.g., the feature review in the American Passionist family monthly, *The Sign,* May, 1977, as well as serious notices in scholarly journals. De Satgé concluded his address of February 10, 1976, on this soaring note: "It seems to me that our Lady stands in the life of her Son's people as a gracious hostess, making one free of large rooms which hitherto had been closed or dark and forbidding. She is supremely fitted to do this, being wholly one of us, and wholly yielded to God, the Mother of God who through grace is the daughter of her Son.

May evangelicals who rejoice in her Son's Gospel take their proper share in calling her 'blessed,' who accepted so fully that grace by which they live."

THE THOUGHT OF ROSS MACKENZIE

Dr. J. A. Ross Mackenzie, Scottish-born and Presbyterian-raised, professor of Church history at Union Theological Seminary, Richmond, Virginia, is an expert on early Christian writings and also on Calvinist origins. He is an associate of the Mariological Society of America and of the Ecumenical Society of the Blessed Virgin Mary, both the parent English Society and the American offshoot. He has taken part in the consultations between Presbyterians and Roman Catholics, and published among other writings noteworthy articles on patristic and ecumenical themes affecting the study of the Virgin Mary, the most recent being the paper he presented at the January, 1978 convention of the Mariological Society of America, "The Patristic Witness to the Virgin Mary as the New Eve" (in *Marian Studies,* 29 (1978) 67-78). In an address he gave in Washington, D.C., April, 1976, "Mary as an Ecumenical Problem" (since published in *Ephemerides Mariologicae,* 27 [1977]) Mackenzie began by describing the current ecumenical revolution as a movement from diatribe to dialogue, and outlined some Marian matters of dispute. To early Calvinists, such as John Knox of Scotland, Catholic veneration of the Virgin Mary seemed idolatrous, a principle of faith and practice Presbyterians carried to the New World. In Mackenzie's words, "Mary was formally separated from Protestant worship and prayer in the 16th century; in the 20th century the divorce is complete. Even the singing of the Magnificat caused the Puritans to have scruples." Although Calvin urged his followers to venerate the Mother of the Lord, in practice the Virgin Mary became the identifiable symbol of Catholicism, sign of everything the Reformers rejected in their positive goal of centering all on Christ, his gospel and his sacraments. In the process even Mary of the Bible and of the primitive creeds was left out.

Mackenzie called for a modern *metanoia,* a "turning of the heart." "To be true to the Reformation does not mean to echo in our day the legitimate protests of Luther and Calvin and those who came after them. "No Popery" and "no Mariolatry" may make popular battle cries, but to be truly "reformed" . . . means to listen afresh to the Word of God as a reality higher than any of our traditions, as that which judges us and our past, and calls us into a new future. A reexamination of the meaning of Mary may well form part of this larger *metanoia* which Protestants, at their best, have always sought."

The Virgin Mary may be a crucial domain in which Catholic and Protestant interests coincide. The question of Mary has taken on new significance in a world that must not forget the Holocaust, Hiroshima and human liberation. We must face the full implications, social and economic as well as religious, of the Magnificat. The witness of Mary is that God is mindful of his mercy; through Christ, in the power of his Spirit, God calls all human beings to dignity, to renewal, to Christian fulfillment. When the down-trodden, whether by race or economics or sex, say Yes to their humanity by affirming what they are, their "Yes, let it be" is an expression among us of the reconciling act of God in Christ.

Near the end of his address of November, 1975, the speaker went back to early Christianity to quote a Mass prayer of the late fourth century, possibly written by St. Basil of Caesarea. It comes from the Coptic Liturgy, and St. Athanasius, patriarch of Alexandria (d. 373), may have used it in the conservative liturgy of the Egyptian Church.

"Remember . . . O Lord . . . especially the holy and glorious
Mother of God, Mary-ever-Virgin; by her prayers have mercy
on us all, and save us for the sake of the Holy Name, which
we invoke." The current second eucharistic prayer in the
revised Roman liturgy is similar: "Have mercy on us all.
Make us worthy to share eternal life with Mary, the
Virgin Mother of God, with the apostles, and with all your
saints who have done you will throughout the ages. May we
praise you in union with them and give you glory through
your Son Jesus Christ."

On December 7, 1977, as the Catholic University of
America, Washington, D.C., celebrated the patronal feast of
the Immaculate Conception, President Clarence Walton gave
the President's medal to Dr. J. A. Ross Mackenzie, in appreciation of special services to the study of and devotion to the
Virgin Mary. Previous recipients had been Archbishop Fulton
J. Sheen, Sister Mary Claudia Honsberger, I. H. M., and Fr.
Théodore A. Koehler, the Marianist curator of the Dayton
Marian Library. At the end of the Mass in the crypt Church
of the National Shrine of the Immaculate Conception, Dr.
Mackenzie acknowledged the medal with a speech of acceptance, which he titled with a phrase from John Calvin, "Let
us now learn to praise the holy Virgin." His remarks were
three-fold: first was that Mary was blessed in the transforma-
tion of our human nature. Taking the occasion of the Catholic feast he asked how we might re-think Mary's Immaculate
Conception so as to deepen our common insight into the
meaning of redemption, a suggestion made recently also by
the Anglican theologian John Macquarrie in the expanded
second edition of his widely-used *Principles of Christian
Theology* (New York, 1977) and in another book as well
(Christian Unity and Christian Diversity, Philadelphia, 1975).

What is fundamental in the Immaculate Conception is
not the precise language Pius IX used in the definition of
1854 but that God's grace seized Mary totally in his redemp-

tive love. Christ has conquered the ultimate enemy, death, both physical and spiritual. Dr. Mackenzie said, "In Galilee the moment came when one among human kind heard God call, 'Where are you?' And in a town in Galilee she answered: 'Let what you have said be done to me.' At that word and out of the whole experience of her life she appropriated the atonement wrought by Christ's passion and received beforehand the empowering of the Holy Spirit. Mary's faith leaps, as it were, across time to share in the salvation given by the life, death and resurrection of her Son.' The holiness God wrought in Mary, his Spirit accomplishes thereby for all human nature: the good news is that only powerlessness like Mary's opens the way to the mystery of the presence of God our strength.

Mackenzie's second point was "Mary, blessed in her openness to God's word." "The Mary who bound herself to the power of God in Galilee did so with every atom of her being . . . She shows us what it means to listen from the heart to God – really to be carrying the Word, to take God's Word into herself, into her body; to give that Word form and shape within her own being; and to give that Word out for the life of the world."

Point three was "Mary, blessed as our particular friend." He quoted the Irish monk, St. Columba (6th century), of the famous Scottish monastic island of Iona, "Think of the dead as though they were your particular friends." Although prayer for the dead is officially disapproved in the Reformed Churches the heart has its own hungers unsatisfied by severe formulas, and Mackenzie gives the example of the seventeenth century writer Richard Baxter, "Calvinist of the Calvinists," who at the death of his beloved wife Margaret in 1681 wrote a beautiful hymn on the communion of saints, that begins, "He wants not friends that hath thy love . . ." Mackenzie commented: "Margaret loved him, and she loved God even more. And Margaret, being Margaret, would not cease to love, even beyond death. If Richard had his Margaret in the communion of God's saints, did he, and do we not also have Mary? 'In the same family we be, by the same faith and Spirit led.' Mary loved Jesus above all; and at the cross Jesus loved too the son she beheld in John. And Mary, being Mary, does not cease to love, even beyond death. Mary does not cease to love the friends of Jesus. 'By the same faith and Spirit led' — she is called with us to an eternal inheritance, linked with the apostles and prophets, a Virgin loved through the favor of our Lord, in the truest sense 'the fruit and the purchase of his passion.' "

THE ECUMENICAL SOCIETY OF THE BLESSED VIRGIN MARY

In the English-speaking world the single most important ecumenical endeavor regarding the Virgin Mary is the Ecumenical Society of the Blessed Virgin Mary, founded in England in 1967. When Mr. H. Martin Gillett, one-time Anglican divinity student and longtime convert to Catholicism, now a retired school-master, first made the proposal, many tried to dissuade him on the ground that the matter of Mary was still too sensitive for unified Christian concern. With the help of friends from various churches, the Society was begun and has enjoyed a healthy growth, spreading to a number of cities in England where regular meetings are held, London, Oxford, Birmingham, Glastonbury, Coventry, Canterbury and others, with members in other countries as well. The Ecumenical Society of the Blessed Virgin Mary of the United States began in 1976, inspired and assisted by the original Society, and has been meeting twice a year in Washington, D.C., on Baptist and Russian Orthodox premises as well as Catholic ones. Three international conferences have been held in England, London, 1971, Birmingham, 1973 and 1975. Cardinal Suenens addressed

the 1971 meeting, as he recalls in the chapter on our Lady
in his book *A New Pentecost?* (New York, 1975, paperback
edition, 1977).

The purpose of the Ecumenical Society is "to promote
ecumenical devotion and the study at various levels of the
place of the Blessed Virgin Mary in the Church, under
Christ." "Devotion" is put first; the phrase, "devotion to
Mary," is avoided as unacceptable to some Protestants. Mary
is related to the Church and subordinated to her Son (*in* the
Church, *under* Christ). Membership is open to "all who are
willing to give support to a Society with these declared aims,
in the cause of Christian unity."

The international conference at Birmingham, Easter week,
1975, took as theme "God and Mary: the Place of the Mother
of the Savior in God's Plan of Salvation," and its eight papers
were published under the editorship of Edward J. Yarnold,
S.J., now co-secretary of the English Society, as the Summer,
1975, supplement to the Jesuit magazine *The Way.* These
papers can serve as an index to the ecumenical variety of the
work of the Society, which has published some twenty-five
conferences given over the years in its own pamphlet series,
and many lectures by its members have been printed in
other journals as well.

Dr. Alasdair Heron of Edinburgh opened the 1975 conference. Speaking from the Calvinist tradition, he said the
title of his talk, "Predestination and Mary," was another way
of phrasing the conference theme, "God and Mary," for
God's plan of salvation is predestination, and the meeting
was about Mary's place in the divine plan. Predestination
points to God's initiative in all things, while Mary stands for
the response of creation to God. Predestination represents
a downward movement from God to human beings; Mary
represents an upward movement to God; where do they
meet? Heron's answer was, "In Christ." In the person and
work of Christ we find God's action of predestination in its

perfection; the history of Christ illustrates the interaction
of predestination and creaturely freedom. Divine action and
human response are at their most perfect in Jesus the Savior.
Our Lady shows also the creature so carried along by divine
initiative that her freedom is in no way lessened.

Father John McHugh (author of *The Mother of Jesus in
the New Testament,* New York, 1975) gave a paper, "On
True Devotion to the Blessed Virgin Mary." He noted that
even ordinary religious words have different meanings for
Protestants and Catholics, even "religion" and "devotion."
Popular piety even more than doctrinal diversity often
stands in the way of Christian reunion. Another way of
putting this, as the American Congregationalist Douglas
Horton (d. 1968), an observer at the Council, put it, is the
inherited "folkways" that divide us, visceral reactions so
deeply hidden as hardly to be susceptible to disinterment.
In his private diary, under May, 1847, John Henry Newman
wrote, "The doctrine of honor to St. Mary and the Saints
brings out a *class of feelings* unknown to Protestants. Hence
the difficulty of talking to them about it."

McHugh recommended Pope Paul VI's letter *To Honor
Mary (Marialis cultus,* 2 February 1974) as a warm and open
and ecumenically helpful exposition of Catholic Marian devotion. He concluded with a quotation from Dante, recalling
how in *Paradiso* the poet passed from the study of theology
through the practice of the virtues into contemplative prayer,
until finally the Blessed Virgin shows him the vision of God.
For she is full of grace and only through grace do we come
to that blessed vision. In the panel discussion that followed
McHugh's presentation, taking the floor, as he noted, after
a Catholic bishop, an Anglican abbot, and an Orthodox
archimandrite, the Methodist Marcus Ward (d. 1978) said
that when McHugh wound up with the Dante quotation,
"I was almost there — I felt like standing up and shouting
out the Magnificat, saying, 'Praised be God.' and going

home!" Ward pleaded for joint study of Mary's role in the
communion of saints as indispensable to ecumenism.

Jack Dominian, the Catholic psychiatrist, spoke of the
formative influence of Mary on Jesus. "The Relationship
between Christ and Mary." Mary's trust gave her Son the
means of trusting himself and reaching others also. Jesus
gives no evidence of having a possessive mother, quite the
opposite. Nor does he show any shyness with respect to the
bodily and the sexual: the Gospels depict our Lord in a re-
laxed relationship with women from all walks of life.

The American Ecumenical Society of the Blessed Virgin
Mary met for the first time in April, 1976. H. Martin
Gillett, founder and general secretary of the English Society,
was guest at the April, 1977 meeting in Washington. The
November, 1977, meeting was held in the First Baptist
Church in Washington, and an ecumenical prayer service
was held there in early 1978. The spring 1978 meeting of
the Society was in the Russian Orthodox Church in
Washington. Papers have been given by a number of mem-
bers and guests: Ross Mackenzie, F.M. Jelly, O.P., Arthur
Crabtree (Baptist), Reginald H. Fuller (Anglican), Orthodox
theologians John Meyendorff and Alexander Schmemann,
E.R. Carroll, O. Carm., and Dr. Mary Carroll Smith. So far
the only American publication has been the paper the president of the U. S. Society read at the April, 1977, meeting:
Donald G. Dawe (Union Theological Seminary, Richmond,
Va.), *From Dysfunction to Disbelief. The Virgin Mary in
Reformed Theology.* (Along with information about
membership in the Society and notices of its meetings, Dr.
Dawe's pamphlet can be had through the Ecumenical Society
of the Blessed Virgin Mary, Box 4557, Washington, D.C.
20017). Dr. Dawe's title, *From Dysfunction to Disbelief,*
is a sort of inversion of the old axiom that the pattern of
praying goes hand in hand with the pattern of believing (the
Latin *lex orandi, lex credendi*). From the neglect of the

Virgin Mary in Reformed piety there came a falling-off also of beliefs affecting her. Dr. Dawe's conclusion is: "She still stands before us, through the witness of Scripture, as the Mother who bears and protects her Son. Just as in her womb and in her home she bore and protected her Son from the forces of a despising society and a murdering king, she now bears and protects the mystery of his being in our midst. Without her the redemptive mystery of her son is lost. With her it is received with joy."

The Holy Spirit
and the Virgin Mary

IN MAY 1975 two international meetings were held in Rome:
a Catholic charismatic congress and a congress on our Lady.
At the Marian meeting a French Dominican spoke about the
Holy Spirit and the Blessed Virgin in the light of the charismatic renewal, beginning his address by saying that one con-
spicuous sign of the work of the Holy Spirit today is the re-
discovery of the person and proximity of Mary. The American Bible expert, Fr. George T. Montague, S.M., gave this
personal testimony in *Riding the Wind* (a Pillar paperback,
Pyramid Publications, New York, 1977), which has a chapter, "Mary and Learning the Ways of the Spirit," "The
experience of Mary . . . is one of the most precious gifts of
the Spirit. She is a charism of the Spirit in person. From her
I learn to believe more purely, to discern the Spirit more
clearly, to listen to the Word more intently, and to await
more creatively the hour of the Lord's coming."

In his 1974 letter on Mary Pope Paul called for exploration of the bond between Mary and the Holy Spirit. Ancient
Christian authors developed scriptural insights in seeing
Mary as "fashioned by the Holy Spirit and shaped into a new
creature" (no. 26 in *Marialis cultus,* no. 56 in *Lumen gentium,*

the constitution on the Church). Medieval writers attributed
to the Holy Spirit "the faith, hope and charity that anima-
ted the Virgin's heart, the strength that sustained her acceptance of God's will and the courage that upheld her in her
suffering at the foot of the cross" (no. 26).

The custom grew among Christians of calling on our
Lady "in order to obtain from the Spirit the ability to en-
gender Christ in their own soul," and the Pope quoted St.
Ildephonsus of Spain (d. 667), "a prayer of petition, power-
ful in expression and content":

Virgin Mary,
hear my prayer:

Through the Holy Spirit
you became the Mother of Jesus;
from the Holy Spirit
may I too have Jesus.

Through the Holy Spirit
your flesh conceived Jesus;
through the same Spirit
may my soul receive Jesus.

Through the Holy Spirit
you were able to know Jesus,
to possess Jesus,
and to bring him into the world;
through the Holy Spirit
may I too come to know your Jesus.

Imbued with the Spirit,
Mary, you could say:
"I am the handmaid of the Lord,

be it done unto me according to your word";
in the Holy Spirit
lowly as I am, let me proclaim
the great truths about Jesus.

In the Spirit
you now adore Jesus as Lord
and look on him as Son;
in the same Spirit,
Mary,
let me love your Jesus.

(translation by Bro. Valens, F.M.S., Sydney, Australia)

Study of the Holy Spirit, not only by theological
scholars, but also by those engaged in pastoral ministry will
"bring out the hidden relationship between the Spirit of God
and the Virgin of Nazareth, and will show their influence on
the Church. From a more profound meditation on the truths
of the faith will flow a more vital piety" (no. 27).

In the conciliar decree on the missions (1965), after
saying that Jesus sent his Spirit from the Father that the
Church might grow, the bishops continued, "For it was from
Pentecost that the Acts of the Apostles took their origin. In
a similar way Christ was conceived when the Holy Spirit
came upon the Virgin Mary. Thus too Christ was impelled
to the work of his ministry when the same Holy Spirit des-
cended upon him at prayer" (no. 4). In two of the three
sendings of the Spirit mentioned by the Council the Virgin
Mary was present, at the Annunciation and Pentecost. The
Gospels do not speak of her presence at the baptism of
Jesus in the Jordan.

The first stage took place in the virginal womb of Mary.
By the power of the Holy Spirit she conceived the unique

Mediator who came to give not an exterior law, as with Moses on Mt. Sinai, but to give his Church the very Spirit of God. Pentecost began the third stage of the saving design, the missionary enterprise of the Church, as the apostles gathered with Mary in the upper room to receive the Holy Spirit. The life of Jesus began with the Spirit overshadowing Mary, the life of the Church began on Pentecost with the Spirit overshadowing the new family of Jesus.

When the Spirit is received, there is a surge of joyful activity, the spreading of the "good news." For the 500th anniversary of the Augustinian Shrine of Mary, Mother of Good Counsel, Genazzano, Italy (1467-1967), Father S. Lyonnet, S.J., French scripture expert, wrote an essay about our Lady and the Holy Spirit, with this reflection, "We know what the 'good advice,' the 'good counsel' was that the Spirit of her Son suggested to his mother at the moment of the incarnation in her virginal womb: 'Thereupon Mary set out, proceeding in haste in the hill country . . . ' " The effect was the sanctification of Elizabeth's son, John the Baptist. "By the intermediary of Mary he was 'filled with the Holy Spirit in the womb of his mother' (Luke 1, 15), as the angel had promised doubting Zachary, 'he will be filled with the Holy Spirit from his mother's womb.' "

In the Gospel of St. John, the wedding at Cana took place the same week as Jesus' baptism, the first week of the new creation for St. John. In the first part of this chapter we considered the similarities between the beginning of the Acts of the Apostles and the "opening sign of Cana" by which Jesus manifested his glory and his disciples believed in him, describing the wedding feast as a "pentecostal meditation." The Spirit comes when men and women take Jesus at his word. At Cana Mary said, "Do whatever he tells you." Jesus said, "Fill the jars with water." St. John reports, "They filled them up to the brim." In the Acts of the Apostles the Spirit comes upon the assembly gathered in obedience

to the parting command of the Risen Jesus. At both Cana
and Pentecost the result is fulness beyond human expectation: the best wine in overflowing capacity, "filled to the
brim'; on Pentecost, as Jesus had promised ("not by measure
does the Father give the Spirit" John 3, 34), they were all
filled with the new wine of the Spirit (2, 2; 2, 4; 2, 13), as
Joel had prophesied (2, 17, Peter's Pentecost sermon).

In the early seventies the experts of the French Society
for the study of our Lady devoted three meetings to the
Holy Spirit and the Virgin Mary. The Sulpician A. Feuillet
studied the role of the Holy Spirit in the infancy narratives
and in St. John. All three evangelists, Matthew, Luke and
John, regard the role of the Spirit as bringing into being the
new people of God, the followers of Christ. St. Matthew
begins his gospel, "Book of the *genesis* of Jesus Christ, son
of Abraham," and continues with the genealogy from
Abraham to Jesus. Even though he gives the genealogy only
back to Abraham, St. Matthew's use of the word "genesis"
recalls creation at the beginning of the Bible, the book of
Genesis, to show Christ as the new Adam in whom the new
creation begins.

God's Spirit hovered over the waters at the first creation;
the Spirit brings about the new creation: this is the significance of the virginal conception of Jesus. St. Matthew repeats the point: "She was found to be with child through
the Holy Spirit" (1, 18), and again in the angel's dream
message to Joseph, "She has conceived what is in her by
the Holy Spirit" (1, 20). Of old the Spirit was promised
to bring about restoration, to give new life to the messianic
land and messianic people, e.g., Isaias 32, "Once more there
will be poured out on us the spirit from above; then shall
the wilderness become fertile land and fertile land become
forest." Ezechiel (ch. 37) prophesied about the dry bones
stirred into life by God's power, his spirit making them
living persons again. Now the activity of the Spirit, so

dramatically demonstrated in the conception of Jesus, achieves the appearance of the new people of God, the body of Christ, the Church.

Gabriel's words to Mary of Nazareth, "The Holy Spirit will come upon you," occur again in the words of Jesus in Acts, "You will receive power when the Holy Spirit comes upon you" (1, 8). Like St. Matthew, St. Luke regards the virginal conception of Jesus as a sign of the new creation, the new era of grace. More than St. Matthew St. Luke stresses Mary's consent, and what she consents to is the creation of the new people of God by the Spirit.

Gabriel promises Mary, "The Holy Spirit will come upon you, and the power of the Most High will cover you with his shadow." "Power of the Most High" is biblical language. Isaias wrote of "the pouring out of the spirit from above, from on high" (32, 15). St. Luke puts Jesus before us as the promised Messiah; the outpouring of the Spirit comes through Christ. At the end of the Gospel the Risen Jesus speaks to his disciples in the same way as Isaiah, "Stay in the city then until you are clothed with *the power from on high*" (Luke 24, 49). The angel's words, "The child will be holy," have their counterpart in the Acts, "Jesus of Nazareth . . . God anointed him with the Holy Spirit and with power" (10, 38). The power of Jesus consists in·possessing the Spirit.

A common role of the Spirit in the Bible is prophecy, that is, the communication of God's word for the needs of the prophet's own day, sometimes with a projection into the promised future. Messianic prophecy is the result of the action of the Spirit in the cases of Zachary and Simeon in St. Luke's gospel. At the Annunciation, however, the Spirit appears in his recreating role. The Christian temporal reckoning, A.D., *anno domini* ("in the year of the Lord") began with Gabriel's greeting, *Ave Maria* ("Hail Mary"). The Godspell, the "good news" began with the Angelus. Isaiah

had prophesied the Spirit from on high would turn waste-
land into fertile soil; now the Spirit from on high is poured
out to effect the virginal conception of Jesus. God has come
among men, Emmanuel, so that, led by the Spirit, Jesus
may form for himself the body which is his Church, the
promised messianic people.

St. John's description of the death of Jesus is, "When
Jesus took the wine, he said, 'Now, it is finished.' Then he
bowed his head, and delivered over his spirit" (19, 30). The
crucifixion and death of Jesus is also his hour of triumph.
In New Testament thought, particularly in St. John, only
when Jesus has been glorified, in his victorious return to the
Father (7, 39) can he send his Spirit. The reference to the
Savior's death is much more than that he "expired," "breathed
his last," "gave up his spirit." The translation of the New
American Bible, "delivered over his spirit," expresses the
sending of the Holy Spirit.

The presence of the "woman," Mary, mother of Jesus, at
her Son's cross, and the Savior's words, "Woman, there is
your Son," and to the "disciple whom he loved," "There
is your mother," are part of the victory of Calvary. Like
Matthew and Luke St. John is concerned with messianic
maternity, with the Church as new "mother of the living"
(the meaning of the name "Eve" in Genesis 3, 20); the motherhood of Mary prepares for and makes possible the motherhood of the Church. As the English Benedictine Henry
Wansbrough described the giving of Mary to John's care and
her adoptive motherhood of the beloved disciple, "It is the
climax of Jesus' deeds on the cross, the climax of his 'hour',
because it sets the Church on its path, creating the community of love between those he loves" (as quoted in the
U.S. Bishops pastoral, *Behold Your Mother* no. 37).

Father Heribert Muehlen is a German theologian who
published his first studies on our Lady and then became
deeply involved in the theology of the Holy Spirit. He

wrote that Mary stood on Calvary, herself receiving the
Spirit as archetype for the whole priesthood of believers.
"Insofar as from the hour of Christ's death, his Spirit has a
history in the Church, first manifest at Pentecost, we can
say with Hans Urs von Balthasar that the Church as a subject
begins to be present in Mary, and is perfected through the
mystery of the Holy Spirit. Mary at the cross is the archetype of all those who after her will be the bride of Christ in
the Church." Mary is herself a member of the Church, joined
to her Son by her pilgrimage of faith on earth, joined now
to the Risen Christ, and in both stages under the influence
of the sanctifying Spirit. Her merciful role is totally sub-
ordinate to the Holy Spirit.

According to H. Muehlen and others, the Second Vatican
Council did not present a well-developed theology of the
Holy Spirit, yet did give some good insights on the Holy Spirit and the Church, e.g., in *Lumen gentium,* on the Church,
"In order that we might be renewed unceasingly in him
(Ephesians 4, 23), he shared his Spirit with us. This Spirit
exists as *one and the same in the head and the members* and
gives life, unity and motive power to the whole body" (no.
7; emphasis added). The underscored words bring out an
often neglected aspect of the Church, i.e., the Church is not
only the "body of Christ," which can be misunderstood as if
the Church "swallowed up" individuals in the interest of
unity, but also the "people of God" and especially "the bride
of Christ," standing over against Christ the Bridegroom. The
Church and the Incarnation are not synonyms, but different realities; it is the role of the Holy Spirit, bond of love,
both to perfect individuality and to unite Head and members
in one body.

According to Muehlen the Second Vatican Council supplied needed correctives to Catholic piety towards the Mother
of Jesus by relating her properly to the Holy Spirit. Even
though Mary is called "most gracious advocate," as in the

familiar prayer, the "Hail, holy queen," it is important to
bear in mind that the Holy Spirit is the great Advocate in the
Church, promised by Jesus at the Last Supper (John 16, 7).

The relationship between Mary and the Church shows
that no one biblical image exhausts the mystery of the Church.
"Body of Christ" from St. Paul conveys the mystical identity
between Christ the Head and his members, the sons and
daughters of the Church. Other scriptural images, as people
of God and bride, bring out the distinction between Jesus
and his followers. A good instance of this is the ecclesial
understanding of the Assumption of Mary, called by the
Council "a sign of sure hope and comfort for the pilgrim
people of God," sign and achievement of the response of
the Church, bride of Christ, to the Bridegroom's invitation.
In celebrating the Assumption of Mary the Church cele-
brates herself as Bride of Christ called to glory.

Catholics who become acquainted with charismatics from
the Protestant and Pentecostal traditions have encountered
the ecumenical problem of Marian devotion. The charismatic movement in its American origins early in the twentieth
century grew out of strong Protestant roots, and it is not
surprising that people of such a decided Reformation background should have very different outlooks on the Virgin
Mary than Catholics. For some Catholics, the charismatic
renewal has meant a rediscovery of Mary as the Spirit-filled
woman of the Gospels; for others, contacts with Protestants
and Pentecostals have led to an embarrassed silence about
the Virgin Mary or a playing down of the role of our Lady
in the communion of saints.

A number of Catholics engaged in the charismatic renewal
have written about our Lady and the Holy Spirit, e.g.,
Cardinal Suenens (*A New Pentecost?* and other writings),
Father Heribert Muehlen, whose thoughts can be found sum-
marized in the article, "New Directions in Mariology," in
Theology Digest, 24 (Fall, 1976) 286-292. A remarkable

testimony by the American ecumenist, Kilian McDonnell, O.S.B., appeared in the charismatic magazine, *New Covenant,* March, 1977. Fr. McDonnell writes that his experience in ecumenism had reinforced his "native restraint" with regard to Mary, so much so that when a French scripture scholar suggested he look into St. Luke's Gospel and the first two chapters of the Acts of the Apostles for further light on Mary as herself a charismatic, he did so fully expecting to find his own contrary ideas reinforced. Instead, he made the joyful discovery of our Lady in her intimate bond with the Holy Spirit.

In Pentecostalism, according to Fr. McDonnell, two major spiritual forces are considered "Presence" and "praise." "Presence" means God takes the initiative, seizes us and our whole life, claims us totally. A deeply personal "yes" is the human response to the approach of Presence, and usually takes the form of "praise." Both Presence and praise are true of Mary of the Scriptures: Presence is a capital theme in the Annunciation, "the power of the Most High will overshadow you." St. Luke uses the Presence of God over the ark of the covenant to explain the Presence of the Most High over the Virgin Mary. The ark was the sacred chest which contained the tables of the commandments and other objects of the Jewish religion; it was enshrined in the holy of holies in the temple at Jerusalem. Mary's response to the Presence within her is praise, "My soul magnifies the Lord, and my spirit rejoices in God my Savior." The response of the disciples at Pentecost is similar to Mary's response; in the power of the Spirit both Mary and the apostles declare the "great things" of God (Acts 2, 11; 10, 46), "magnifying" the Lord, and rejoicing.

According to Fr. McDonnell the centuries-long experience of Mary in the liturgies of East and West offers ecumenical enrichment. Christians are encouraged to make the most of their liturgical riches to celebrate Mary's holiness in the

Spirit. The witness of Mary should not be overlooked in considering New Testament teaching on Presence and praise; the Virgin Mary has a charismatic role. Mary, in the Scriptures and in traditional Christian celebration, is the ark of the Presence and the singer of praise.

Part II: Questions on Mary

THE VIRGIN MARY AND ECUMENICAL DIFFICULTIES AND HOPES.

Alan Gill: Pope Paul VI once expressed his personal sorrow that his own office, that of pontiff, should be a cause of disunity rather than unity among Christians. Would you feel that our Lady is also a cause of disunity, and as an ecumenist, do you see a change in this situation?

Eamon Carroll: Your question is a good one. Our Lady, as the Mother of the Lord, is not personally a cause of disunity; she has to be regarded by any thoughtful Christian as herself a cause of unity. However, Catholic attitudes towards our Lady do clash with attitudes of other Christians towards her. So if your question were to be rephrased, "Is what a Catholic holds about the Mother of Jesus a cause of difficulty, a factor that impedes unity between Catholics and other Christians?", then I would say yes, that is unfortunately true.

The dialogue format adopted in this section of the book is most suitable to focus our attention on problems and questions which are of current interest to many people and which often perplex others. The author is especially thankful to Alan Gill, the religious editor of the *Sydney Morning Herald,* who drew up the questions which he thought were most pertinent.

AG: Is the situation changing for the better?

EC: I think so. Slowly, however. I don't think there is any dramatic breakthrough; but there are signs of a new interest, of amicable interchange between Protestants and Catholics on this sensitive issue, and that itself is a good sign. It would be an exaggeration to say that there has been a tremendous explosion of ecumenical interest in the Virgin Mary even on the level I happen to know best, which is the scholarly level. In terms of the grass roots I am not qualified to say, but it seems we are a long way still from achieving a unity about this sensitive question. Is that precise enough?

AG: Yes.

EC: The movement is by no means abortive; the baby has been born but is still very small, in terms of ecumenical concern. When I say "concern," I do not mean simply study, I mean a praying concern on the part of Christians to appreciate the true role of the Mother of Jesus.

AG: You obviously feel that the role of our Lady need not be divisive.

EC: Certainly not. It seems to me that any Christian, Protestant or Catholic, man or woman, older person or younger person, who takes the Scriptures seriously will meet the Mother of Jesus, who was near the cross of her Son on Calvary, who was at the wedding feast of Cana with its symbolism of Church unity and of the messianic times that have finally come, who was committed to the will of the Father. Recall her words at the Annunciation, so like the phrase of the Our Father, "Behold the handmaid of the Lord; be it done unto me according to *your* Word." Anyone considering these facts in the scriptures can appreciate that the

Mother of Jesus has one will with her Son and shares his prayer at the Last Supper, "Father, I will them to be with me whom you have given me," his prayer for Christian unity. So it is a problem of Christians misunderstanding her, of Catholics being overly polemic at times in their advocacy of her; of Protestants, because of things that happened at the Reformation, holding back too much from an appreciation of what was a common patrimony. So far as Mary herself is concerned, I regard her as a factor of unity.

AG: It has occurred to me that greater study of the communion of saints could lead to an ecumenical approach, both to the subject of intercession in general and the role of Mary in particular.

EC: You put your finger right on the heart of the differences, and touch also the possibility of a gradual appreciation of the present place of the Mother of the Lord. What happened at the Reformation was that in reaction to excesses in the period prior to the Reformation, all the great Reformers without exception — Luther, Calvin, Zwingli, Bollinger and others — uniformly forbade calling upon the saints in prayer, including the Mother of Jesus, even though these reformers continued to hold a great veneration for the Mother of the Lord, as is evident from their writings. They felt that to call upon the saints in prayer, even the Mother of Jesus, was to show a lack of confidence in the great Intercessor who is the Risen Christ. In this extreme reaction, as some of their latter day followers are now willing to admit, they broke with the tradition of understanding of the present role of the Mother of Jesus and of the saints, in union with the Risen Christ, a tradition coming from the early Church.

If those who have fallen asleep in the Lord — our parents, please God, if God has taken them already, our friends, the good people who have lived in the centuries before us, all

our ancestors, our friends who have died in the war, and died
in accidents, and died of old age, etc., if all these people who
have fallen asleep in the Lord are with the Lord, why should
it not be possible, as the Church believed uniformly in the
West up to the Reformation, as the Catholic Church, many
Anglicans, and the whole Eastern body of Christians still
believe, why should it not be possible to call on them for the
same sort of help that we call upon each other for? No
Christian doubts the possibility and the legitimacy, the
desirability, of asking others for help. Many religious people,
even those who do not honor Christ as God, believe in the
power of prayer. They believe in God and ask each other
for prayers. They do not view the prayers that others say
on their behalf as in any way blocking their access to Christ
who is the supreme intercessor, the one unique Mediator.

It is Catholic belief, consistent with pre-Reformation
tradition and shared with the whole body of Eastern Christians, the majority of whom do not possess a Roman alle-
giance, that calling upon our friends for help in prayer ex-
tends beyond the barrier of death, and that those we know
to have been close friends of God, above all the Mother of
Jesus, the perfect Christian, the closest disciple of Christ,
are still in a position to help us. This is the most sensitive
issue in the differences about the Virgin Mary between
Protestant and Catholic, most sensitive because it touches
not merely belief and doctrine, but touches practice also.
If I were a Protestant looking at Roman Catholic piety toward the Virgin Mary, the most evident aspect of what
Catholics hold about our Lady would be that they pray to
her. A whole pattern of piety is built around Roman '
Catholic practices of devotion to the Virgin Mary. There
are other significant differences also. Some doctrines
Catholics hold about the Mother of Jesus, that she was free
from original sin, which goes under the name of her Immaculate Conception, that she is now, body as well as soul,

in union with the Risen Christ, which goes under the some-what difficult word "Assumption," are real difficulties. The most basic difference, however, because it is open to every-day observation, is devotion to Mary, particularly "praying" to the Virgin Mary.

One of the questions put to me in ecumenical gatherings over and over again is the place of the Virgin Mary in the communion of saints, why Catholics pray to Mary and the saints. If we could first begin to understand what each side really holds about this and why it holds it, then perhaps in God's good time we could achieve some sort of consensus. I am convinced we are dealing here with something that belongs to basic Christian understanding and practice and that the protest of the Reformation in this respect was extreme.

AG: You have just touched on a point concerning definition of terminology. I have heard at times Catholics speak of Mary in poetic terms, in effect the language of love. I have heard it said that good poetry makes poor theology.

EC: I don't agree to that judgment. The language of devo-tion is the language of love and it may not be suitable for a rigorous theological discussion, but there is no reason why things people believe should not be expressed in beautiful language. I suppose one must say that the language of poetry is not the precise language of the theologian. But the theologian is not just making a human construct, he is not just building his own castle of words with scientific terms, he is dealing with truths, matters of faith, what he believes, and the belief of the Church body in which he stands. To express this in lovely language, in the language of poetry, is not only a good thing, it is necessary. What one might do in a classroom and what one might do in a pulpit, what one might do on a festal occasion and what one might do in the rigor of a scholar's library do not call for the same words.

AG: But it would make poor theology in the sense that a poet uses poet's license.

EC: Ah yes, fair-enough. A good example of that, which many persons conversant with good English will recognize, is the writing of Newman of the last century, the famous John Henry Newman, important figure in the Oxford Movement, who became a Catholic about the middle of his long life. His scientific writing, his historical writing, his careful, logical, lucid writing is beyond reproach; he was also a brilliant poet and a marvelous preacher who could go from one to the other without difficulty, respecting the peculiar type of discourse in which he was engaged, whether it was a university lecture or a talk to ordinary people, or poetry. I don't think there is any necessary clash.

AG: I understood though that Newman actually objected to the poetic approach regarding Mary.

EC: He objected to the poetic approach associated with Southern European countries. He was not personally warm to Italian types of manifestation of devotion to the Virgin Mary. They didn't suit his temperament, as he admits clearly. He found some of these devotional writings intolerable, particularly as translated from Italian into English with a profusion of superlatives which good English does not use. His own writings, for example, *Meditations and Devotions,* which was published posthumously, many of them written for the poor people of Birmingham, are filled with tenderness, but in an English style which is different from Spanish or Italian style. (Editorial addition: Newman's awareness of the difference between the language of popular devotion and the precise words of doctrinal definitions is demonstrated drily in a famous essay of July, 1859, "On Consulting the Faithful in Matters of Doctrine," "I have always fancied that, when Catholics were accused of hyberbolical language towards the Blessed Virgin, it was replied that devotion was not the measure of doctrine: nor surely is the vernacular of a magazine writer.")

AG: Many Protestants find objectionable the Catholic view that Mary is the gentle Mother, more lenient, more compassionate and understanding than Jesus Christ. She appears to be used as a means to manipulate God, taking him by the weak side, as it were. I believe that St. Alphonsus Liguori saw God as an irate corrector whose woeful arm was withheld only by the prudent and tender-hearted Virgin.

EC: Well, certainly St. Alphonsus did not hold that. I do not doubt that there are ill-instructed Catholics who do regard the Mother of Jesus as a sort of "go-between" to a stern Christ, but in no way is that Catholic teaching. It verges on travesty. To think that I as a Catholic do not have direct access to Christ, who is not only my judge but also my merciful Redeemer, to think that I need the Virgin Mary as a merciful "go-between" to a stern and remote Christ, that is not Catholic teaching. That impression is sometimes conveyed and I regret that. It is surely not Catholic understanding.

AG: It would be defended by many Catholics.

EC: Maybe some would defend it; if so, I would be the first to tell them they're wrong. Our Lady in her earthly life was totally open to the will of God; that is the biblical picture of her and does not require any rigorous demonstration. Catholic teaching is that now her will is still completely one with the Risen Christ. There is no clash between a will of mercy

that would belong to the Mother of Jesus and a stern judgment that would belong to her Son; that's absurd. If there
are Catholics who hold that, they simply are wrong. How
widespread such a view would be, I honestly don't know. I
know I have encountered occasionally something close to
that on the part of ill-instructed people, but I do not think
it is widespread and I would certainly hope that it is not.
And if a Protestant, rooted in Christ, correctly holding the
centrality of Christ, encounters this and feels that this is
Catholic piety to our Lady, he has every right to resist it,
because he is resisting something that's wrong.

AG: What of St. Alphonsus writing of Mary as the tender
intercessor before an angry God?

EC: St. Alphonsus Liguori is sometimes quoted that way,
but St. Alphonsus Liguori was a careful theologian, whose
life was centered on Christ and who understood Christ as
the merciful Redeemer. What is often quoted from him is a
book, often not printed fully, called *The Glories of Mary,*
which is widespread and which includes popular stories. But
St. Alphonsus was not foolish. He uses stories as we use
stories, but gives explanations that make it clear the mercy
of Mary is an aspect of the mercy of Christ. It cannot be
otherwise.

AG: Touching on your own ecumenical involvement, I have
noticed that modern theological books by Roman Catholic
scholars often avoid the phrase "the Mother of God". In
conversations with me and at one of your public lectures,
you used the term "Mother of Jesus". Do you feel that
there is a misunderstanding about these definitions?

EC: I do, and I am glad you asked it. In my public talks
I frequently do use the term "Mother of Jesus" because

often my talk is biblically centered. Our Lady in the Scriptures is "the Mother of Jesus," the phrase used by St. Luke and St. John."Mother of God," which I accept fully, is a term that was sanctioned, solemnly defined by the Council of Ephesus in the year 431, the Third Ecumenical Council. It was so proclaimed not primarily to give greater glory to the Mother of Jesus, but to bring out the truth that the Son of Mary was the Son of God. Therefore, the Mother of Jesus can legitimately be called the Mother of God, given, of course, the mystery that God became man. Obviously, she cannot be called Mother of God in the sense of existing before God; that would be not only blasphemous but absurd.

The term "Mother of God" had been used in prayers in some portions of the Church, at least one hundred years before Ephesus. It comes from a Coptic setting, and was in use in Egypt. St. Athanasius, defender of the faith of the Council of Nicea (325 A.D.), who lived through most of that century, uses the term "Mother of God" in his writings. It was defined by Ephesus in the year 431 and then became a part of liturgical prayer. After Ephesus it was inserted, e.g., in the Eucharistic prayer, where it still is, in the East and in the West. Luther uses the title "Mother of God" and Calvin holds the truth of the divine maternity; as I recall, he did not use the exact term, but there is no question but that Calvin held that what is conveyed by the term "Mother of God" is true of the Virgin Mary.

AG: They used the exact term?

EC: Yes, "Mother of God," or the Greek "theotokos." The normal English equivalent for a Catholic is "Mother of God." Many an Anglican would say "the God-Bearer," which is more accurate, but I find it a little gauche as English. Subsequent to the Reformation, many Protestants came to feel "Mother of God," though a legitimate term used at Ephesus to defend the truth about the Son of Mary, that He is indeed Son of God, took to itself some corruptions of the goddesses of the Mediterranean world, so that instead of remaining an accurate, conciliar term, it became debased in popular piety. Therefore in an ecumenical setting, I usually say "Mother of Jesus." But when I celebrate the Liturgy, as in daily Mass, I say "Mother of God." "Mother of Jesus" is the more biblical term, and when I am speaking of Mary in the Bible, in her historical setting, "Mother of Jesus" is the indicated term.

THE IMMACULATE CONCEPTION AND THE ASSUMPTION: SENSE AND PROSPECT.

AG: The two Marian doctrines that have aroused most controversy in recent times have been the Immaculate Conception and the Assumption. Would you please explain what is meant by those terms?

EC: We mentioned a while back that one of the difficulties in dialogue between Catholics and other Christians is a difference of terminology. It is almost impossible to overemphasize how urgent is the task of finding common language, or, if we cannot find common language, at least to appreciate what words mean in the other religious tradition. In the case of these two Catholic doctrines, the Immaculate Conception and the Assumption, we face an unusually formidable language difficulty. The term "Immaculate Conception" is easily misunderstood and confused with the truth of the virginal conception of Jesus, which goes normally under the phrase "virgin birth," meaning that Jesus did not have a human father, that the mother of Jesus, the Virgin Mary, conceived Jesus her Son, the Son of God,

without a human father. That is the "virgin birth" or the
virginal conception, which is part and parcel of the faith of
all Christian churches, I would suggest; it goes back to St.
Matthew's gospel and to St. Luke's, to the ancient creeds
and to Reformation professions of faith also.

The Immaculate Conception is a completely different
thing; in Catholic understanding, the mother of Jesus was
conceived and born of two human parents like all of us. What
it means is that from the instant she began to exist as a human
person in her mother's womb, she was so graced by God, so
filled with God's love, as to be free of original sin; therefore
her passive conception, her coming into existence as human
person, was a sinless coming into existence, was an immaculate conception. I must confess that if I were a Protestant,
I do not think that would be immediately evident to me
from the term "Immaculate Conception."

The Assumption is another difficult religious word because in ordinary usage an assumption is an unproven hypo-
thesis. We have here a highly latinized word that has come
over into English. What it means *literally* is a taking up, a
lifting up, a raising up; what it means *in fact,* as a doctrine,
is that the Mother of Jesus, at the end of her days on earth,
was united with Christ her Son in heaven, in glory, in the
fullness of her personality. Fullness of personality means,
in our understanding of a human person, body as well as
soul. The Assumption is the mystery of the fullness of God's
grace, the grace of Christ come to achievement in the Virgin
Mary.

The Immaculate Conception means that at the beginning
of her existence as human person, the most remote beginning, in the womb of her mother, Mary, the child of two
human parents, whom ancient books, though not the scriptures, call Joachim and Anne, was so filled with the love of
God, by his gracious gift, as to be kept free of original sin.
The Assumption says that at the end of her days on earth,

Mary was united body and soul with Christ her Son.

AG: Can it be said that the doctrine of the Assumption has nothing to do with the body of our Lady and does not necessarily mean that our Lady was, before or after death, physically carried up into heaven?

EC: Let me try to sort that out and give you a fair answer. The doctrine was defined only in 1950 by Pius XII but has been held by Christians from the sixth century. It is the oldest explicit feast of the Blessed Virgin Mary; it was celebrated as early as the sixth century, homilies survive from that period. The doctrine, not only as defined but long before it was defined, holds that the Mother of Jesus, as whole person, therefore body as well as soul, body-soul composite, is united now with Christ the Risen Savior. Now the further question: does this mean her body was taken up? It means that the whole person of Mary is there with Christ.

Further question: does it mean the very body that she had here on earth and that died, as seems more likely? The scriptures are silent about how our Lady ended her days on earth, and the definition simply said "at the end of her days on earth." The more indicated view in Christian tradition over the centuries is that Mary died. Does definition of the Assumption, or belief in the Assumption, or celebration of the Assumption, tell us anything about what happened to the body of Mary if and when Mary died? In fact, it does not. The definition of the Assumption simply tells us Mary is in union with the Risen Christ body and soul, as whole person. What type of continuity there is between, let us say, the dead body of Mary and the Mary who is now present, body as well as spirit, with her Risen Son, we do not know. Am I answering your question?

AG: I think so, yes.

EC: We simply do not know. In other words, I believe as a Christian, in the resurrection of the flesh. Christians profess in the Apostles Creed and other creeds that we believe in the resurrection of the flesh. Christian belief is that when we die as friends of Christ, when we fall asleep in the Lord as we say in the lovely phrase of Christian prayer, we shall rise with Christ, that we shall pass to another order of existence, more splendid than the present one so familiar to us, and indeed so dear to us, here on earth. We believe that we shall live as whole persons, as body/soul persons, not just disembodied spirits, that we shall live as body/spirit people, as flesh/soul people in union with the Risen Christ. That does not however commit me as part of Catholic belief to a clear position about any sort of continuity between that cadaver, my cadaver which will eventually be disposed of in some manner or other, and what will be my resurrection body. Do I make myself clear?

AG: I think so. I wasn't so much thinking of what happened to our Lady's body, that is to say, her physical remains in the long-term process, but I wanted to find out what the bodily assumption means by the literal sense of it.

EC: The only way to express the notion of a transfer from this order of reality, which is space and time, suffering and death, to a happy life after death, has been in analogous language, because we have no immediate experience of any form of life other than this one. When we try to describe, even when the scriptures try to describe, the form of life which the Risen Savior lives, we are at a loss for suitable language. We say "lifted up" because we think of that other order of existence as being above us. We would not be likely to say "taken down" rather than "lifted up". "Lifted up" conveys a sense of change to a superior order, a better order, even as in the scriptures. The cloud in both the Hebrew bible and the New Testament, for example, the account of the last appearance of the Risen Christ before Pentecost when Jesus is taken from His disciples in a cloud, is a biblical device to convey a change of state.

AG: Yes, the word "lifted up" is perhaps ambiguous, but what I was really trying to find out is whether the Church teaches that her transfer into heaven was essentially different from other human beings.

EC: We don't know about other human beings. But the Church does know, and therefore professed in 1950 with tremendous solemnity what it had celebrated for 1500 years, that the Mother of Jesus is with her Son, in body as well as spirit.

AG: How about the case of other human beings where the soul has left the body?

EC: Your question leads into quite an area of conjecture, but there are Catholic theologians and other Christian theologians who think that all who have fallen asleep in the Lord are already in union with the Risen Christ, body as well as spirit. That's a tenable position, but really quite hypothetical. When I say quite hypothetical, I'm not saying untrue. It could be at some future time the Holy Spirit will lead the Church, not just the Catholic Church but all Christians, to understand that in the treasures of revealed truth, as part of the revelation of God in Christ through his Spirit, is contained the truth that all who have fallen asleep in the Lord are already one with the Risen Christ. As far as we can tell and try to put it into words, when we die we pass over into an order of reality no longer measured by time, no more than it is confined by space, and all that the Church is saying is that the Mother of Jesus is certainly in this blessed condition already body and soul. Do you understand me?

AG: Yes, I do.

EC: So Mary's Assumption is a paradigm for union with the Risen Christ.

AG: The next point which is the shorter one, actually you have already partly answered it, is that opponents sometimes argue that belief in the Immaculate Conception and the Assumption is unscriptural and conflicts with views expressed in their own lifetime by people who are now saints of the Catholic Church.

EC: Again a good point, and a good question. I'll answer the second part of your twofold question first. Yes, that is true of some saints and indeed, some of the greatest teachers in the Catholic Church in centuries past, St. Thomas Aquinas who died in 1274, St. Albert the Great who was his teacher, St. Bonaventure who lived in the same period, St. Bernard (d. 1154) who was the great troubadour of our Lady, none of these men held for the Immaculate Conception. They did not see how they could because it did not seem to make our Lady herself redeemed, and there was only one Redeemer and all people need redemption. The ultimate solution the Church accepted was that there was an anticipatory redemption in our Lady's case, the Immaculate Conception was a preventive redemption.

This doctrine gradually emerged in the Church's consciousness, passing through a period of denial and challenge before it was clarified and finally affirmed. There is no clear scriptural evidence for it, no more than there is clear scriptural evidence for the Assumption. The most that can be shown, at least the most that has been shown thus far, even by the most vigorous protagonists of the Immaculate Conception or the Assumption, is that they are not anti-scriptural . One interested in this problem might go back to just before the 1854 definition, and read in Cardinal Newman's writings his comments on development of doctrine, which are still among the best ever written, and in magnificent English. Newman takes as a prime example of the development of doctrine, not the Immaculate Conception though he was to write about that later, and not the Assumption, though he writes about that also at times, but the early Church's growing conviction that Mary remained always a virgin. This is not demonstrable from scripture but came to be held by everyone, let's say by the year 400, as an early example of the development of doctrine; it became a sore point in interpretation between Protestants and Catholics at a much later time. So it is a question here of development of doctrine within the Church that really owns the scriptures, if I may put it that way, for the Bible is the book of the Church.

AG: There are those, e.g. Anglicans, who believe that the doctrines of the Immaculate Conception and the Assumption are possible or even probable but who query the value of solemn public definitions on these topics. I understand some Roman Catholic theologians also share this view, while obviously accepting the truth of the doctrines themselves.

EC: There are certainly some Roman Catholic theologians who wonder whether it was opportune to define these truths in the style and words chosen for the definitions in 1854 and 1950 and who, all the same, as good Catholics, have accepted them. It is equally true that there are Anglican leaders and others as well, some of whom I have met and whose works I have read, who have no basic quarrel with either doctrine but who wonder why they were defined, as they think, in a rather one-sided way by the Church of Rome.

What's done is done. The Roman Church is not going to rescind them and I really do not think any other Christian group seriously expects it will. What has been suggested, however, on both sides of the ecumenical divide is that further elucidations might be supplied of these doctrines, that more efforts might be made from the Roman side to explain precisely what they mean. That is not too difficult a task, it seems to me. But even more is required and this is more difficult – to show how they fit into the total pattern of Christian belief.

In the decree on Ecumenism which was published at the end of the third session of the Second Vatican Council, on November 21, 1964, the very day on which the dogmatic constitution on the Church was promulgated with its long eighth chapter on the Virgin Mary in the mystery of Christ and the mystery of the Church, reference is made to an "order or hierarchy of truths" (no. 11). of the Catholic faith in proportion to their relationship to the foundation of the faith. The foundation of the faith is Christ himself. That Catholics engaged in ecumenical dialogue should do so not only with charity and openness, but also with a clear consciousness of the order or hierarchy of truths, has been hailed by Protestant leaders, Oscar Cullmann among them, as the single most significant statement among the entire body of the documents of the Second Vatican Council.

Interestingly, in Paragraph 20 of the same "Decree on Ecumenism," where reference is made to things that unite and divide Western Christians, after citing a Trinitarian and Christological formula of faith which is biblical and almost in the very words of the World Council of Churches profession of faith of New Delhi of 1961, the Council then went on to recognize serious differences between Roman Catholic beliefs and beliefs of other Christians with respect to the Incarnation and the Redemption, and therefore with respect to the ministry and mystery of the Church and with respect also to the role of Mary in the plan of salvation. What is being said is that there is an order of truths; the central truth is perhaps to be thought of as the center of a circle, and is Christ Himself, the richness of God's revelation of Himself in Christ in the power of the Spirit. Arranged in concentric circles around the center are other truths of the faith, that are all equally true if God has revealed them, but not all of the same importance. As a Catholic, I do not have the slightest difficulty in saying, indeed I feel obliged to say, that I do not regard the Immaculate Conception of the Virgin Mary or her Assumption as being of the same importance as the truth that Jesus Christ is the savior. Here we have a marvelous platform for serious ecumenical thought and reflection and prayer. Catholics, sensitive to their ecumenical obligations and even to their need to understand better what they themselves profess and celebrate, must go into these matters more. So I think what the Anglican leaders to whom you refer were suggesting can be taken very seriously by Catholics.

THE CATHOLIC TERMS AS "MEDIATRIX OF GRACE" AND "CO-REDEMPTRIX"

AG: During the Second Vatican Council some Roman Catholics hoped and many Reformed Christians feared that our Lady would be declared co-Redemptrix or Mediatrix of all graces with Jesus Christ. To many non-Catholics these terms are offensive. What are the meanings of these terms, and why were they rejected?

EC: It is quite understandable that any Church body should have its own special language. What is unfortunate is that this language can seem so strange to other Christian Church bodies as to be a cause not simply of wonderment but of offense. In the case of recent religious terms, and both of the terms you refer to are comparatively recent, Co-Redemptrix and Mediatrix, these words apparently have struck fear and dismay into the hearts of many sincere Protestants. You asked about the Second Vatican Council. It is true to say that there were Catholics, a fair number among Bishops at the Council, who hoped the Council would consider and possibly define, in other words declare as revealed truth, that our Lady was Mediatrix of grace, or Mediatrix of all graces, or another slightly different way of putting it that comes to practically the same thing, that Mary is Co-Redemptrix, along with Christ the Redeemer.

What do these terms mean, what did the Council do, and why did it do what it did? Why, since the Council, have these terms become infrequent in Catholic use, so that this ecumenical offense has virtually disappeared? The words are Latin terms simply carried over into English, which is an initial inconvenience. The inconvenience is the greater in that Christians, all Christians, with St. Paul certainly regard Jesus Christ as the one only Mediator. Paul says that clearly in his first Epistle to Timothy (chapter 2, v. 5). It would seem to many Reformed Christians that to call anyone else a Mediator, or if that person is a woman, the Mother of Jesus, to call her Mediatrix, is to fly in the face of the biblical insistence that Jesus Christ is our one Mediator to the Father. The term Co-Redemptrix is perhaps even more difficult, in that it would seem to many a Protestant who has not had a chance to look into the matter or had it explained, that it reduces Christ to being half of a team of redeemers. So there would then be a Redeemer and a Redemptrix. Actually, the Latin word "Co-Redemptrix" is clear enough, it means *"with* the Redeemer" and the subordination and dependence of the Mother of Jesus with respect to Jesus Christ, the one Redeemer, is expressed in the Latin. Obviously, it is not so conveyed in English. If you speak of a co-signer on a checking account, the co-signers, say a husband and wife, have

equal rights over the checking account, so "co" means equal
rather than simply "with" or dependent. In Latin the "co" is
"*cum*" ("with"), and does convey the sense of dependence.

Now what does it mean; apart from the words, what do
these concepts mean? What they mean in Catholic understanding is that our Lady was joined to the saving work of
Christ in a responsible fashion, that during the days of her
earthly life the Mother of Jesus was so associated with her
Son's saving work as to have a part in it, that her free and
responsible consent when God asked her to be the Mother
of the Savior, her consent to everything the Father asked
of her in her involvement with her Son through his public
ministry from Cana to Calvary and beyond, where we find
her at the beginning of the Acts of the Apostles praying
with the Apostles for the outpouring of the Holy Spirit, that
all of this was an involvement of our Lady in her Son's
saving work, always in total dependence upon him, always
in terms of walking a way of faith, what the Council called
"her pilgrimage of faith."

In Catholic understanding — and this gets us back to the
earlier topic of the *present* place of Mary in the communion
of saints — our Lady's fellowship with the Risen Lord is such
that she still has an active and loving concern for the rest
of us, the brothers and sisters of Christ. Christ is the first-
born of many brethren. We believe that as Christians we are
the brothers and sisters of Christ, and Mary's concern is that
all of us, all the children of God become more like Christ
who is her first-born, and the first-born into eternity in the
Resurrection. She continues to do that by what we call
technically her intercession, which means that she is an
advocate, a spokeswoman for us, even as we ask others to be
intercessors here on earth by asking them for prayers. That
is the Catholic understanding of the meaning of Mediatrix.
Did the Council deny this? The Council certainly did not
make much of the term "Mediatrix"; it uses it one time only,

as one of a series of terms used to describe our Lady. It does not use the term "Co-Redemptrix" at all. One might say, "well then, does it not seem that the Church of Rome during the Second Vatican Council reversed itself? If the term 'Mediatrix' and to a lesser degree 'Co-Redemptrix' had been in considerable use in Catholic prayers from the early 1920's, as both terms had been, and the Council all of a sudden is so sparing in its use of such language, does it not seem that the Council has cut back on this conviction?" It cut back on the terms, no question of it, but I do not agree it cut back on the conviction. The Council did feel these terms have a certain pastoral difficulty as well as an ecumenical difficulty, by which I mean there is a possibility that Catholics would misunderstand such language, although the ecumenical difficulty is far greater.

What the Council said instead, in its very first decree, which has been described as a sort of seminal document of the entire Council, the decree on the Liturgy, (December 4, 1963) in paragraph 103, was that "the Mother of Jesus is inseparably joined to her Son's saving work." In this setting, what is being said in simple words which are not ecumenically offensive is that Mary, during the days of her earthly life in her pilgrimage of faith, was so open to God's saving will that she was associated to her Son's saving work to the degree that it was possible for her and to the degree that God intended; and that now, because her Son's saving work is an ongoing thing, she is still associated to that saving work in the communion of saints. The scriptures remind us that Christ lives forever to make intercession for us. In Christian understanding the Risen Jesus continues his saving work; it did not conclude when he died on Calvary.

The Council sought to eliminate some of the ecumenical offense it saw in the language of Roman Catholic piety that had become increasingly strong from the early 20's, and found another way of conveying the same truth that would not give ecumenical offense, and be more clear for Catholics themselves. This does not mean that a Reformed Christian can in good conscience accept either part of the statement that our Lady is inseparably joined to her Son's saving work; a Reformed Christian may well have a different understanding of how our Lady was involved in her Son's saving work during her earthly life than Catholics have, and find it difficult to accept the Catholic outlook on how our Lady is now involved in her Son's saving grace.

AG: Wouldn't it have been better to have used some other word, other than "co-," that is, "co-redemptrix?"

EC: Yes, the term "co-redemptrix" lends itself to misunderstanding. When you say "co-redemptrix," you may also say "co-redeemer," as two equal parties, and of course that's not it. The trouble with Latinized words is that if you have no Latin background there is no way of understanding that the Latin background protects the term. And "co-redemptrix" is probably the most stunning example of that. The term is completely avoided by the Second Vatican Council, and was not used even by Pius XII, who was an enthusiastic partisan of Marian devotion.

AG: You mentioned words used by the Second Vatican Council.

EC: The liturgy constitution says, "Mary is inseparably joined to her Son's saving work" (no. 103). That leaves open questions of how she is joined to her Son's saving work. It would be naive to suggest that simply because of a new statement has been made by Rome, it is going to be acceptable to a Reformed Christian. But at least the possible or real ecumenical offense of an extraordinarily difficult term has been put aside.

MARIAN DEVOTIONAL PRACTICES, PRIVATE REVELATIONS AND APPEARANCES AND SIMILAR QUESTIONS.

AG: You made the point to me in our previous conversations that Catholic theology regarding Mary was obscured by what you called Mediterranean-type devotional practices tinged with superstition. Would it be fair to regard as superstitious such practices as the crowning and bejewelment of statues and the alleged miraculous powers of medals and scapulars?

EC: It depends upon those who use them, very often; if people are so ill-instructed as to attach magical qualities to legitimate forms of devotion, then they have become bad for them. But the use of statues, or the decoration of statues, or the carrying of medals or scapulars or other objects of devotion, such things are not of themselves evil. I am not a married man but if I were I would surely carry pictures of my wife and children; I do carry a picture of my mother. That I should want to be reminded of Christ himself, as the cross or crucifix reminds me, or that I should want to be reminded of the Mother of Jesus, as a medal or statue of her, or the scapular, reminds me; these things help me to pray and have confidence in her and I cannot regard this as superstitious.

AG: There is also an apparent belief in the powers of these objects.

EC: Well, if that be true and where it be true, then it is wrong. They are not charms, they are not amulets, they are not articles that have any intrinisic value of their own; they are reminders. In Catholic language, they are sacramentals. They do not have the power of the sacraments, they were not instituted by Christ, but the Church of Christ in its own understanding sees them as objects of piety that reminds us of more basic things.

AG: So what you're saying is that these objects ought not to be regarded as having power in themselves.

EC: Absolutely not, and if I haven't said that already, thank you for putting it in such clear words. They have no power in themselves. They serve as reminders, they are tokens, they are signs, and that's their utility.

AG: Some popular devotional writing on Mary seems to many to contain indications of a mother cult almost distinct from Christianity and occasionally of what one might consider a repressed sexuality on the part of the authors. Do you think that is a fair point?

EC: The point is certainly worth considering and it's worth posing as an objection, and I suppose it is possible to assemble clinical evidence that for some people that is the case. I can't contest that, if it can be shown; I do not think it is generally true, however. It seems to me from my own experience, from my childhood and from the many Catholics I know and have taught and have talked to that their attitude toward the Mother of Jesus is an attitude of sharing in Christ's own veneration and respect for his mother, that there is no sense here of a mother complex or a sexual sublimation because of some inadequacy in their own sexuality. That such dangers may obtain I don't deny, but I think they are aberrations and are rare.

AG: This one will interest you, it's very topical. A suggestion by younger clergy that devotion to our Lady in the past has been "excessive" or "exaggerated" is invariably

counted by statements from others that Mary cannot be
honored too highly and that the neglect of such devotion
is a factor in the Church's apparent decline. There appears
to be almost a gulf on this point. Do you have any views
on this?

EC: Your question touches on a very complicated situation
because you are touching on the whole malaise, the whole
difficulty the Catholic Church has been experiencing since
the Council, a period of self-questioning, a period of doubt,
a period of the falling-off of some old forms of piety, a
period of fewer boys going on to become priests and brothers,
of fewer girls going on to become Catholic sisters. It has
been a very difficult ten years, and that devotion to the
Virgin Mary should be caught up in this time of unease is
not surprising, given that devotion to our Lady loomed so
large in Catholic piety prior to the Council.

Were one to have been told in, say, the year 1960 that a
Council was about to be held (it had been announced by
that time) and that after the Council there was going to be
a great time of trial, a clairvoyant person (few people seem
to have been) might have expected that in such a time of
upheaval, one of the areas where it would be manifest
would be devotion to our Lady, precisely because she had so
big a place in Catholic piety, and this is precisely what has
happened. I do not regard the difficulties and the fall-off in
devotion to our Lady as causing the malaise, I think it is a
reflection of it. What we have here is a bit of feed-back,
where one is the cause of the other, the other the cause of
the first. The two are so interwoven they are inseparable.
It is simplistic to say only that one is the cause of the other.
Both are happening simultaneously because both are part of
the same reality. With regard to the axiom you quoted,
"Never enough about our Lady," or "One cannot say too
much about our Lady," I agree. I also say it is possible to

say wrong things about her. One cannot ever say too much of the truth about her because one can never have too much of the truth, but certainly one can have exaggerations and one can have inadequacies, and simply multiplying inadequacies is not praise. So, if the axiom be taken correctly, no quarrel with it; but if it be taken in an abusive way, I'd have to quarrel with it.

AG: Some of the more conservative among the women's groups in the Church have suggested a possibly surprising role for Mary as the first true, (as opposed to the trendy) "women's libber," and that the Pope himself has spoken equivalently.

EC: Pope Paul did offer Mary as a model to modern woman. This letter merits respectful hearing because it is filled with good things and comes from a very open mind and heart. The letter on the right order and promotion of Marian devotion is dated February 2, 1974. It is an unusual Roman document in many ways, not least in its remarkable clarity. I don't mean that Roman documents are deliberately obscure, but often enough the style in which they are written is difficult to translate and makes hard reading. They are often rather technical documents; this is not. It is a wonderful pastoral, in the good sense of pastoral. In this document, the Pope suggests that the Virgin Mary is a model for modern woman in her legitimate aspirations to take her proper place in society, and he gives good examples of it. He is saying that woman cannot be limited to the home and to the Church, that she has a big role in modern society; there is a true freedom of woman, and Mary is the model of this. How? Well, surely not, he says, in terms of the limited social circumstances of her own day.

The young girl, the young wife, the young mother of Nazareth, lived in a social setting that is not an ideal and cannot be reproduced in any case. It is part of history. In terms of openness to God and response to God's will made manifest in daily life and in the crises the gospels bear witness to, her role in the infancy of Christ and his childhood, her role at Cana, her role in the public life where she appears as the model of those who follow Christ, her role on Calvary, her role before Pentecost, in this Gospel sense she is an example of openness to God and to neighbor. That is an ideal of true liberation of women. I do not think it is simply conservative women who are saying this, I think many Christian women, by no means just Catholics, have found this in our Lady's life and in what the Scriptures tell us about her. Her Magnificat is a hymn of liberation. There is a sense of real adult responsibility before God and before neighbor. A lot can be done with that.

AG: These last three points are inter-related. In recent years there has emerged a number of outwardly loyal Catholic organizations which combine Marian devotion with biblical prophecy, theories about Satanism and Communism, and belief in an imminent Armageddon. These organizations claim loyalty to the principles of the Catholic faith and they are largely based on the visions of Fatima. What is your view of these organizations?

EC: There are such organizations all around the world, they tend to be what I would call the "radical right." They are ultra-conservative; they feel and say in their literature that only they have the correct understanding of Catholic faith and practice, that unless one views the Mother of Jesus in the way they do, often much bound up with private revelation, the viewer is mistaken, doesn't have a correct view and authentic understanding of our Lady and devotion to her. I cannot accept that limited outlook of "the radical right." They have over-reacted defensively to the changes in the

Church, to good changes as well as to frightening things
that have happened within the last ten years, where good
people have been caused suffering by rapid changes that
have left them in the lurch. Some of these very conservative groups have reacted to form private enclaves, little
groups who feel they are the only ones protecting the truth,
that they have secret access to truth, including a correct
understanding of the Virgin Mary. Often publicity makes
them look bigger than they are. In the long run, it seems to
me, many of them will collapse of their own weight. I am a
little apprehensive about them because I feel by their propa-
ganda they do harm sometimes to others, but overall I do
not think they swing that much weight, at least in the
general Catholic community. With respect to Fatima, which
comes into that —

AG: That is my next question. The visions of Fatima are
regarded as authentic by the Church. On the one hand there
is the suspicion that it is bogus, and on the other some think
that it is too fearful to be revealed, caused by Pope John's
refusal to reveal the contents of what is claimed to be our
Lady's third and final message at Fatima. Will you comment
on that?

EC: Again, it's a rather complicated question. Let me state
initially the position of the Catholic Church with respect
to private revelation. The private revelation was the alleged
appearance of our Lady (and "alleged" is not passing judgment on my part) to three children in Fatima, in Portugal,
in 1917. There were a series of such appearances in that
year, in which our Lady asked for prayers and penance and
made certain promises, among them that the war would
soon end, and eventually the conversion of Russia. The
Church has approved this event only to this degree, namely:
the devotions that have sprung up there, and indeed around

the world, under the name of Our Lady of Fatima, are good devotions. The Church has said, "We see prayer and penance, we see people practicing works of charity, we see people going to the sacraments of penance, and the Eucharist, and these are good things." In Roman Catholic understanding, such a judgment of the Church is protected from error because these are means by which people live their Christian lives and practice their faith.

With respect to the claims of the children (one of these children is still alive, a nun called Sister Lucy) to have seen a vision of our Lady, the most the Church will say, indeed the most the Church *can* say is that it is worthy of human faith. In other words, I could be a good Catholic and not accept Fatima. I could not say that the devotions practiced there are bad devotions, because the Church has passed judgment on that. But with respect to the events that were the occasion of the beginning of these devotions, the pilgrimages and practices of prayer and penance, I could be in total communion with the Church, be an excellent Catholic and also a devout client of the Virgin Mary and say, "Well, Fatima doesn't get through to me." Do I make myself clear?

AG: Yes, you do.

EC: With respect to some of the subsequent events that are incorporated in your question, the so-called secret of Fatima, the letter that was not to be opened until 1960 and that apparently Pope John and others decided was not to be revealed to the Church, whatever may have been in it, the most that could be of any significance and the most that the Church could give a judgment about that would be free of error would be some reminder of things we have forgotten as Christians, which really comes back again to the basic gospel teaching of prayer and penance and the sacraments and love of God and love of neighbor. Human beings are curious, and I do not except myself from that statement, so we are fascinated by a secret letter or private revelation that seems to hold promise of some further opening into the mysteries of God and things we do not know. Yet in Catholic understanding there cannot be any new gospel, there can be nothing hidden from us that we now need to know in order to be good Christians, and true followers of God.

AG: I take it then that it is not part of Catholic teaching, or not necessarily a part of Catholic teaching, that it is to be kept a secret?

EC: No, absolutely not; not only is it not part of authentic Catholic teaching but it cannot be. The most the Church will do — even at Lourdes, which is much better known, the events that gave rise to the Lourdes pilgrimages took place in 1858, well over a century ago, and Lourdes really has had an enormous echo in the entire Catholic world — the Church says no more than that the events that gave rise to the pilgrimages are worthy of human faith. So I could be a good Catholic and not be convinced of Lourdes. Let me add, though I am quite convinced.

AG: But the Church says the acts of piety there are good; what of the initial events?

EC: Yes, as far as human investigation can show, there has been no fraud. In other words, with respect to Fatima, the local bishop and the Roman See have sent investigators there, highly trained people who have made a study of this sort of thing, they have interviewed the witnesses and what they say rings true. But it rings true in terms of human testimony. That is what I mean when I say it's not fraud. Get hold of the letter put out by the American bishops called *Behold Your Mother Woman of Faith;* there is a

section in it on the meaning of private revelation, which
expresses what I have been trying to say here, and makes the
distinction between what is of lasting value and obligatory
and what is free matter. I am not pressing obligation in this
answer, but making a distinction between what the Church
says I must accept as a Catholic and where the Church simply
says We've looked into it, sent investigators, and as far as we
can see it is true. [Editorial addition: here are the paragraphs from the joint pastoral of the bishops of the United
States concerning private revelation:

"We turn our reflections now to the authenticated appearances of our Lady and their influence on Catholic devotion especially in the years since the Apparition at Lourdes,
in 1858. Other 19th century events of this kind were the
experiences of St. Catherine Labouré in 1830 (the Miraculous Medal), and the apparition at La Salette in 1846. In
our own hemisphere we recall the apparition in 1531 of Our
Lady of Guadalupe, 'Queen of the Americas.' Best known
of the 20th century appearances of the Mother of the Lord
is that at Fatima, in 1917.

"These providential happenings serve as reminders to us
of basic Christian themes: prayer, penance, and the necessity
of the sacraments. After due investigation, the Church has
approved the pilgrimages and other devotions associated with
certain private revelations. She has also at times certified
the holiness of their recipients by beatification and canoniza-
tion, for example, St. Bernadette of Lourdes and St.
Catherine Labouré. The Church judges the devotions that
have sprung from these extraordinary events in terms of its
own traditional standards. Catholics are encouraged to
practice such devotions when they are in conformity with
authentic devotion to Mary. Even when a 'private revelation'
has spread to the entire world, as in the case of Our Lady of
Lourdes, and has been recognized in the liturgical calendar,
the Church does not make mandatory the acceptance either

of the original story or of particular forms of piety springing from it. With the Vatican Council we remind true lovers of our Lady of the danger of superficial sentiment and vain credulity (the phrase of the Constitution on the Church, n. 67). Our faith does not seek new gospels. but leads us to know the excellence of the Mother of God and moves us to a filial love toward our Mother and to the imitation of her virtues (also as in the constitution on the Church, N. 67)" (numbers 99 and 100 from *Behold Your Mother Woman of Faith,* 21 November 1973)].

AG: Yes, well this leads me to my very last point. What is your opinion of the alleged visions of Mary at Garabandal and La Salette, and of the movement founded in Spain by Archbishop of Hue, Viet Nam?

EC: I known nothing about the last item, Viet Nam, and please forgive my ignorance. La Salette (1846) has been well investigated and is worthy of human faith. About Garabandal, I know of three or four independent teams that have gone there and all said "no go," no evidence of anything more than human, no evidence of an appearance of our Lady. The Bishop there has consistently forbidden people to go there. That is the present position of the Church.

AG: The Church did not put Garabandal on a level with Fatima?

EC: Completely the opposite.

AG: La Salette?

EC: La Salette would be on the level with Lourdes though it never became as popular. If you read about La Salette

(1846) there are difficulties, but overall it rings true and certainly the practices of prayer and penance have been salutary and wholesome.

Part III: A Selective List
of Recommended Readings
on the Blessed Virgin Mary

THE LIST of recommended readings on Mary is deliberately long — to offer a wide choice from the enormous amount of excellent writings on the Blessed Virgin, from sources in England, Ireland, Australia, Canada and the United States, and even other countries. In some instances, materials listed will not be available except in major libraries, e.g., scholarly journals like the quarterlies *Marianum* from Rome and *Ephemerides Mariologicae* from Madrid, proceedings of congresses, national and international, and lesser known magazines. It has been thought desirable, all the same, to list such items to show the subject has received serious attention. Most items are recent, within the last ten years. All entries are written in English, even if the essay is in a book with a foreign language title.

Certain standard references are so indispensable to the serious inquirer that the question arose whether to list the full contents; the choice was not to do so, but only to make a selection. For example, in the *New Catholic Encyclopedia,* plus its supplements one and two (volumes 16 and 17), the reader is reminded that most of the articles on Mary are in volume nine, but the cross-references and the index lead to other articles. The same problem occurred with *Marian Studies,* the annual proceedings of the Mariological Society of America, twenty-nine of whose book-size volumes have appeared, 1950 through 1978, each containing four to six

papers given at the yearly convention, covering a vast range
of materials by well-known scholars in such areas as the
bible, the Fathers, the *magisterium,* medieval authors and
ecumenism. For many years *Marian Studies* took up distinct
themes each year; that gave way to a more catholic choice,
with an increasing ecumenical concern of late years.

In preparing this selective list the compiler used the five
English-language bibliographies that appeared in the sixties
in *The Marian Era,* and the multilingual Survey of Recent
Mariology from annual meetings of the Mariological
Society of America, since January, 1967, printed in *Marian
Studies.* Readers who would appreciate a ten-year run-down
of writings in English and other principal languages will find
it in E. R. Carroll's Theology on the Virgin Mary: 1966-1975,
in *Theological Studies,* 37 (June, 1976) 253-289. For the
general public the unpretentious magazine, *Our Lady's Digest,* founded and edited for many years by the La Salette
Father Stanley Matuszewski, M.S., renders extraordinary
service; it appears every other month, except July-August,
and provides quality materials, both original and reprint, e.g.,
a recent issue has the translation of the Swiss Bishops' joint
pastoral on our Lady, 33 (May-June, 1978) 20-23. A fair
number of the recommended titles in the following pages
are from this inexpensive magazine; full address: Our Lady's
Digest, Twin Lakes, Wisconsin 53181.

THE MARIOLOGICAL SOCIETY OF AMERICA

Marian Studies is the annual proceedings of the Mario-
logical Society of America, containing the papers given at
the annual convention of the Society, held in early
January. The Society began to meet in 1950; the founder,
Rev. Juniper B. Carol, O.F.M., is the secretary of the
Society and editor of *Marian Studies.* Many of the earlier

volumes are still in print, and can be had from Marian
Studies Office, 1600 Webster St. N.E., Washington, D.C.
20017; it is possible to subscribe in advance as well. An in-
dication of contents of the twenty-nine volumes, 1950
through 1978, follows:

vol. 1 (1950): general questions: F.J. Connell, C.SS.R.,
   E. Burke, C.S.P.
vol. 2 (1951): the co-redemption: Cardinal Wright, L. Everett,
   C.SS.R.
vol. 3 (1952): spiritual motherhood: G.W. Shea, C. Vollert,
   S.J., F. Friedel, S.M.
vol. 4 (1953): queenship: Eustace Smith, O.F.M., F. Schmidt,
   O.F.M.Cap.
vol. 5 (1954): Immaculate Conception: A. Wolter, O.F.M.,
   A. Robichaud, S.M., A. Kippes, O.M.I.
vol. 6 (1955): divine motherhood: J. Chiodini, G. Van
   Ackeren, S.J., B. LeFrois, S.V.D., J. Shannon, O.S.A.
vol. 7 (1956): Mary's virginity: P. Donnelly, S.J., G. Owens,
   C.SS.R., N. Flanagan, O.S.M., E. R. Carroll, O. Carm.
vol. 8 (1957): did our Lady die?: W.J. Burghardt, S.J.,
   J.P. O'Connell, T. W. Coyle, C.SS.R.
vol. 9 (1958): Mary-Church: J. F. Sweeney, S.J., F.L.
   Cunningham, O.P.
vol. 10 (1959): principles of Mariology: P. Mahoney, O.P.,
   M. Griffin, O.C.D., W. Hogan, E.D. O'Connor, C.S.C.
vol. 11 (1960): the Gospels: E. May, O.F.M. Cap., S.
   Hartdegen, O.F.M., C.P. Ceroke, O.Carm.
vol. 12 (1961): the Old Testament: B.M. Ahern, C.P.,
   D.J. Unger, O.F.M.Cap., J.T. Forestell, C.S.B., C.
   Stuhlmueller, C.P.
vol. 13 (1962): Spirit of virginity: W.J. Burghardt, S.J.
   (presidential address, The Mariologist as Ecumenist),
   E.H. Maly, A. Tegels, O.S.B.

vol. 14 (1963): Mary's holiness: A. Agius, O.S.B., J.C. Turro, Alban A. Maguire, O.F.M.

vol. 15 (1964): Bishop Austin B. Vaughan, J.R. Aumann, O.P., Thomas A. O'Meara, O.P.

vol. 16 (1965): New Testament questions: C.P. Ceroke, O.Carm., M.B. Schepers, O.P., W.F. Dewan, C.S.P., G. Wood.

vol. 17 (1966): C.J. Wessels, O.P., G.T. Montague, S.M. (Our Lady and Eschatology), W.G. Most, Bernard J. Cooke.

vol. 18 (1967): communion of saints: P.J. Cahill, A.C. Piepkorn.

vol. 19 (1968): liturgy and devotion: J.E. Manton, C.SS.R., A.C. Cochrane, A. Schmemann, P. Sherwood, O.S.B.

vol. 20 (1969): A. Maguire, O.F.M. (presidential), Sister Sean, Sister Rosanne, P. Hinnebusch, O.P., R. Masterson, O.P.

vol. 21 (1970): William J. Cole, S.M. (on Luther), F.M. Jelly, O.P.

vol. 22 (1971): A. Vaughan (presidential), W.G. Most, R. Kugelman, C.P.

vol. 23 (1972): Josephine M. Ford, C.W. Neumann, S.M. (presidential), T. Koehler, S.M., A. Schmemann (Our Lady and the Holy Spirit).

vol. 24 (1973): Mary's virginity: A.C. Piepkorn, H.W. Richardson.

vol. 25 (1974): G.F. Kirwin, O.M.I., T. Collins, O.P. (on scripture).

vol. 26 (1975): Ross Mackenzie, M. Miguens, O.F.M. (Mary's virginity).

vol. 27 (1976): hierarchy of truths: F.M. Jelly, O.P., D. Dietz, O.M.I., P. Kearney (Gen. 3, 15 and Johannine theology).

vol. 28 (1977): J. Reese, O.S.F.S. (gospels), J.T. Ford, C.S.C. (Newman on *sensus fidelium*), W.J. Finan, O.P. (Mariology and ethics), W.A. Marshner (criteria for doctrinal development).

vol. 29 (1978): J.A. Hardon, S.J. (catechetics), R.H. Fuller
(New Testament and Theotokos), R. Mackenzie (new
Eve), J.T. O'Connor (contemporary challenges), F.M.
Jelly, O.P. (presidential).

Each year since 1967 (vol. 18) *Marian Studies* has had "a
survey of recent Mariology," by E.R. Carroll, O.Carm., 1972
(vol. 23) only being excepted, when a report was given instead
of the Zagreb (1971) International Mariological Congress.

THE MARIAN LIBRARY, UNIVERSITY OF DAYTON, DAYTON, OHIO

Marian Library Studies is currently the title of the scholarly annual published by the Marian Library, University of
Dayton, Dayton, Ohio 45469, with articles in English and
other languages. Théodore A. Koehler, S.M. (Marianist) is
the editor. It began in 1969; the latest volume to appear is
volume 8 (1976). In vol. 1 (1969) Brother William Fackovec,
S.M., of the Library staff, contributed, "The Marian Library
of the University of Dayton," and A. M. Allchin, "Mary,
Virgin and Mother: An Anglican Approach." Alexander
Schmemann wrote for vol. 2 (1970) "On Mariology in Orthodoxy." Marian Zalecki, O.S.P., has in vol. 8 (1976) the
doctorate dissertation he defended in May, 1975, "Theology
of a Marian Shrine. Our Lady of Czestochowa."

In September, 1967, the Marian Library concluded a
series of 132 pamphlet reprints of significant articles that
had run for many years, first under the heading of "Marian
Reprints," then as "Marian Library Studies." The Library
also published for a very short period a series of larger bro-
chures, only a few appeared, called "Marian Library Studies."

PUBLICATIONS OF THE ECUMENICAL SOCIETY OF THE BLESSED VIRGIN MARY

The Ecumenical Society of the Blessed Virgin Mary was founded in England in 1967; it now holds regular meetings in a number of English cities, and has members in other countries.

The Ecumenical Society of the Blessed Virgin Mary of the United States began to meet in 1976. The English Society has published some of the conferences given at various meetings, including the three international ecumenical congresses the Society organized, in London, 1971, and in Birmingham, 1973 and 1975. Many papers presented by Society members and to Society gatherings have been published in various journals, and some of the Society's own publications have been printed elsewhere also, occasionally in America. Here is the list of publications to date; most of them are still to be had. For copies and information on membership (which brings the interesting Newsletter, an occasional bulletin) write either the Secretary (and founder) Mr. H. Martin Gillett, 237 Fulham Palace Road, London SW6 6UB or the Associate General Secretary, Rev. Edward J. Yarnold, S.J., Campion Hall, Oxford OX1 1QS.

Ralph Russell, O.S.B., Gordon Wakefield, and J.C. de Satgé: *The Blessed Virgin in the Bible,* and other papers; all three also in *One in Christ,* 4 (1968) 137-164.

Eric L. Mascall: *The Mother of God.*

Bishop W. Gordon Wheeler (Leeds): *The Blessed Virgin Mary and the Post-Conciliar Scene.*

Canon Donald Nicholson: *The English Caroline Divines and the Blessed Virgin Mary.*

Archbishop Cardinale: *Pope Pius XII and the Blessed Virgin Mary.*

Archimandrite Kallistos Ware: *The Mother of God in Orthodox Theology and Devotion.*

Reverend Stewart Denyer: *Magnificat.*

Rev. Gordon Wakefield: *Intercession.*

Hon. Ada Mary Ammon: *Mary, the Gaiety of God.*

Rev. Prebendary H. Cooper: *Mary, the Obedient Woman* (also in *Our Lady's Digest,* March-April, 1972).

C. Stephen Dessain, C.O.: *Cardinal Newman's Teaching about the Blessed Virgin Mary* (also in *Our Lady's Digest,* Jan.-Feb., and March-April, 1973).

Bishop Alan Clark: *Mary's Place in the Ecumenical Dialogue.*

Rev. Richard J. McCarthy, S.J.: *Mary in Islam.*

John Coventry, S.J.: *Mary's Place in Our Redemption.*

Rt. Rev. J.E. Fison (bishop of Salisbury): *The Blessed Virgin Mary in the Sarum Tradition.*

Archbishop Cardinale: *Our Lady and Ecumenism.*

Frederick M. Jelly, O.P.: *The Place of the Blessed Virgin in a Secular Age.*

René Laurentin: *Mary in the Communion of Saints.*

Donal Flanagan: *An Ecumenical Future for Roman Catholic Theology of Mary* (also as "Mary in the Ecumenical Discussion," in *Irish Theological Quarterly,* 40 (July,1973) 227-249).

Rabbi Nicholas de Lange: *A Woman of Israel.*

Bishop Alan C. Clark: *The Holy Spirit and Mary.*

John C. de Satgé: *The Evangelical Mary.*

Ross Mackenzie: *Mary as an Ecumenical Problem* (given to the United States Society, April, 1976; also in *Ephemerides Mariologicae,* 27 (1977) 29-36).

Sebastian Brock: *Mary in Syriac Tradition.*

John Saward: *The Assumption* (with comment by G.B. Timms, Bishop B. C. Butler; a reply by Henry Chadwick is in the Society *Newsletter* for Spring, 1977); also in *Sobornost,* series 7, no. 5 (Summer, 1977).

Bible and Tradition in Regard to the Blessed Virgin Mary,
a one-day conference, October 1, 1977, by Marcus Ward
(Methodist), E. Yarnold, E.L. Mascall and G.B. Timms.

Alberic Stacpoole, O.S.B.: *The English Tradition of the
Doctrine of the Immaculate Conception,* paper given
Autumn, 1977.

Mrs. A.G.C. King: *Living Lourdes,* dated September, 1978.

The papers given at the third international ecumenical
conference, Birmingham, April, 1975, make up the Summer,
1975, *Supplement to The Way* (no. 25), edited by Edward
J. Yarnold, S.J. The following papers are included: *Intro-
duction,* by E.J. Yarnold; *God and the Feminine,* by John
Macquarrie; *The Grace of Christ in Mary,* by Alasdair Heron;
Born of the Virgin Mary, by Bishop Clark; *The Theme of Eve
and Mary in the Early Christian Church,* by J.A. Ross
Mackenzie; *The Relationship Between Christ and Mary,* by
Jack Dominian; *On True Devotion to the Blessed Virgin
Mary,* by John McHugh; *Mary in the Lucan Infancy Narra-
tive,* by Rev. Marie E. Isaacs (Baptist).

The United States Society has so far published only one
conference: by its president Donald G. Dawe, *From Dysfunction to Disbelief. The Virgin Mary in Reformed Theology,* paper given at the meeting in Washington, D.C., of
April 30, 1977: this can be had, and also information on
membership in the Society, announcements of meetings,
etc., from the Society headquarters, Box 4557, Washington,
D.C. 20017.

THE MARIAN ERA

The Marian Era was the yearbook of the Franciscan
National Marian Commission, edited by Marion A. Habig,
O.F.M. The subtitle, World Annual of Queen of the Universe,

described its scope. A large-size volume of 100 to 150 pages, it combined articles by writers of world renown with original art work and reproductions of Marian masterpieces of the past. The publication ran from 1960 to 1974; the publisher was the Franciscan Herald Press, Chicago. A sampling of contents is here given along with list of volumes; items bearing an asterisk were reprinted in the final cumulative volume.

Vol. 1 (1960): Anglican devotion to Mary (J.C. Stephenson); St. Francis and our Lady (R. Brown).

Vol. 2 (1961): Mary and Protestant Concern (P. Palmer, S.J.); Islam and the Virgin Mother (John M. Abd-El-Jalil, O.F.M.)*; St. Lawrence of Brindisi, Marian doctor (N. Sonntag, O.F.M. Cap.).

Vol. 3 (1962): Marian Centres and Libraries (A. Boeddeker, O.F.M.)*; Popes and Immaculate Heart (J.J. Murphy).

Vol. 4 (1963): Pope, Council, Reunion and Mary (M.A. Habig); Recent Biblical Studies (E.H. Maly).

Vo. 5 (1964): Mother and ideal image of the Church (C. Balic, O.F.M.); Dante and Mary (L. Brophy).

Vol. 6 (1965): Newman, Marian doctor of our time (L. Brophy)*; Padre Kino and Our Lady (C.W. Polzer)*.

Vol. 7 (1966): Christian's Exemplar of Faith (M. Donnellan)*; Our Lady of the Portal (H.M. Gillet); Knight of the Immaculate, (Blessed Maximilian Kolbe) (Francis Mary Kalvelage, O.F.M. Conv.).

Vol. 8 (1967): The Spirit of chapter eight in the constitution on the Church (G. Philips); Ancient Prayers to Mary (A. Hamman, O.F.M.)*; The Acathistos Hymn (G.G. Meersseman, O.P.)*; Ecumenical Mariology (Alois Mueller).

Vol. 9 (1969): Origin of Marian cult in the West (H. Barré, C.S.Sp.); From 1854 to Vatican II (G.M. Besutti, O.S.M.); Servant of the Lord (M. Miguens, O.F.M.)*.

120   Understanding the Mother of Jesus

Vol. 10 (1971): Pilgrim of Faith (J. Galot, S.J.)*; Our
Lady's Preacher, St. Bernardine of Siena (Patrick J. Ryan,
S.J.); Oldest prayer to Mary—we fly to thy patronage
(J. Auer)*.
Vol. 11 (1974), cumulative volume, with the full text of
the United States bishops' pastoral, *Behold Your Mother,
Woman of Faith.*

Five of the issues contained an extensive "Recommended
Reading in Mariology," by E.R. Carroll: in vol. 1 (1960), a
first list; in vol. 3 (1962), English Marian Literature, 1960-
1962; in vol. 5 (1964), Recommended Reading . . . 1962-
1964; in vol. 7 (1966), Recommended Reading . . .1964-
1966; in vol. 9 (1969), Recommended Reading . . . 1966-
1968.

CHURCH DOCUMENTS

Marialis cultus, Feb. 2, 1974, in various editions and trans-
lations: E.C.T.S., London, *To Honor Mary;* Devotion to the
Blessed Virgin Mary, in *The Pope Speaks,* 19 (1974:1) 49 –
87. About it: D. Flanagan, The Veneration of Mary: A New
Papal Document, in *The Furrow,* 25 (May, 1974); John
Cardinal Carberry, Marialis Cultus: A Priestly Treasure, in
Homiletic and Pastoral Review, 78 (May, 1978).

Paul VI: some of his many Marian documents: *Signum
magnum* (Fatima anniversary, May 13, 1967), in *The Pope
Speaks,* 12 (1967:3) 278-86; *Christi Matri Rosarii* (rosary
encyclical), of Sept. 15, 1966, in *The Pope Speaks,* 11 Summer, 1966) 221-5; May 1, 1971, to rectors of Marian
Shrines, English in *L'Osservatore Romano,* May 13, 1971,
also in *Our Lady's Digest,* Sept.-Oct., 1971; to the Roman
congress, May 16, 1975, in *The Pope Speaks,* 20 (Winter,

1975) 199-203; Gaudete in Domino (on Christian joy), in
Catholic Mind, September, 1975. On, Pope Paul, S. O'Reilly,
Our Name is Peter, Chicago, 1977, one chapter on our Lady.

John XXIII: Prayers and Devotions from Pope John
XXIII, ed. J.B. Donnelly, Garden City, N.Y., 1969, pb.;
Rosary Meditations, London, 1966, also in *The Pope Speaks,*
9 (1963) 92-99, and *Review for Religious,* 21 (1962) 397-
407, available as reprint as well.

The Documents of the Second Vatican Council are to be
had in a number of editions and translations; the chapter on
our Lady is the final chapter of the dogmatic constitution
on the Church, *Lumen gentium,* Nov.21, 1963, although
significant references to our Lady occur elsewhere also, e.g.,
liturgy no. 103, priesthood no. 18, missions no. 4, lay
apostolate no. 4. Of commentaries, two especially: Donal
Flanagan, in *Vatican II: The Constitution on the Church,*
ed. K. McNamara, London, 1968, Chicago, 1968; Otto
Semmelroth, in *The Documents of Vatican II,* ed. H.
Vorgrimler, vol. one, London, 1967, New York, 1967.
Further: R. Laurentin, The Virgin Mary in the Constitution
on the Church, in *Concilium,* vol. 8 (1965) 155-172; W.G.
Most, *Vatican II: Marian Council,* Staten Island, 1972,
Dublin, 1972, pb.

Dominic Unger, O.F.M.Cap., edited and translated three
major encyclicals: *Mary Immaculate* (Pius IX, 1854), *Mary
Mediatrix* (St. Pius X, 1904), and *Mary All-Glorious* (Pius
XII, 1950), all Paterson, N.J., 1946, 1948 and 1956.

William R. Lawler, O.P., editor, *The Rosary of Mary,*
Paterson, N.J., 1944; sixteen rosary documents of Leo XIII.

Pius XII, Mariology and the Standards which Govern its
Study, in *The Pope Speaks,* 1 (1954) 343-6: *Inter com-*

plures, to a study congress.

W. J. Doheny and J. E. Kelly, compilers, *Papal Documents on Mary,* Milwaukee, 1954: thirty-six from Pius IX to Pius XII.

Papal Teachings. Our Lady (monks of Solesmes), Boston, 1961.

Thomas J. Burke, S.J., ed., *Mary and the Popes,* New York, 1954 (five major documents).

Behold Your Mother, Woman of Faith, November 21, 1973, joint pastoral of the bishops of the United States, Washington, D.C., 1973; also in *Catholic Mind,* May, 1974, and elsewhere. See Eamon R. Carroll, O.Carm., How the Joint Pastoral, Behold Your Mother, Came to be Written, in *University of Dayton Review,* 11 (Spring, 1975).

Lawrence Cardinal Shehan, *Mary Mother of God Woman of Faith,* pastoral of September 8, 1971, in *Our Lady's Digest,* July-August, 1972.

Cardinal Medeiros, *Renewal of Marian Piety,* Boston, 1972 (for May, 1971).

Archbishop P. Pocock, *Mary and the Mystery of the Church,* for May, 1964, in *The Ecumenist,* 2 (May-June, 1964) and *Our Lady's Digest,* 19 (December, 1964) 193-7.

Mary in Philippine Life Today, joint pastoral of February 2, 1975: extensive brochure, 55 pages, from Catholic Bishops' Conference of the Philippines, Manila.

Paul Palmer, S.J., *Mary in the Documents of the Church,* Westminster, Md., 1952.

J. Neuner and J. Dupuis, editors, *The Christian Faith in the Doctrinal Documents of the Catholic Church,* Westminster Md., 1975, pb, first American edition from Jesuit faculties in India, a chapter on BVM.

COMPILATIONS

T. Burke, S.J., editor, *Mary and Modern Man,* New York, 1954; ten essays, as D. Sargent, Our Lady and Our Civilization, and Paul Palmer, Mary and the Flesh.

Juniper B. Carol, O.F.M., editor, *Mariology,* in three volumes, 1, 1955, 2, 1956, and 3, 1961, Milwaukee; vol. 1 mainly on sources, 2 on doctrines, 3 on devotions; many authors and topics: W.J. Burghardt on Fathers, C. Vollert and G. Van Ackeren on various doctrinal points, E.R. Carroll, on magisterial documents and on Marian congresses, G.W. Shea on the rosary, C.P. Ceroke on the scapular devotion.

J.C. Fenton and E.D. Benard, editors, *Studies in Praise of Our Blessed Mother,* Washington, D.C., 1952; thirty-four articles from *American Ecclesiastical Review,* by J.B. Carol, F.J. Connell, T.U. Mullaney, and others.

Donal Flanagan, *In Praise of Mary,* Dublin, 1975, pb.: delightful anthology with excellent comments.

Kevin McNamara, editor, *Mother of the Redeemer Aspects of Doctrine and Devotion,* Dublin, 1959, also New York, 1960, though omitting C.B. Daly's essay on Lourdes and J. Cunnane's on Marian piety in Ireland.

Vincent J. Nugent, C.M., editor, *The Mariological Institute Lectures,* St. John's University, Jamaica, N.Y., 1959, pb: for the Lourdes centenary, 1958, five lectures, e.g., E.R. Carroll on the Assumption, G.W. Shea on the Immaculate Conception.

E.D. O'Connor, C.S.C., editor, *The Mystery of the Woman,* Notre Dame, Indiana, 1956: for the Marian year, W.J. Burghardt's "Theotokos: the Mother of God" has been reprinted in various places, as in the W.J. Burghardt and W.F. Lynch editors, *The Idea of Catholicism,* New York, 1960, also pb.

Frank Sheed, editor, *The Mary Book,* New York, 1950: harvest of 25 years of Sheed and Ward authors.

First Franciscan National Marian Congress, Burlington, Wisconsin, 1952: held for the Assumption, October, 1950; among papers, Noel Moholy, "St. Irenaeus—the Father of Mariology."

Second Franciscan National Marian Congress, San Francisco, 1957: from congress of 1954, centenary of Immaculate Conception definition; N. De Amato, A. Wolter, etc.

Mary in the Seraphic Order (vol. 35 of Franciscan Educational Conference), Chicago, 1954: many topics as Scotus, St. Bernardine, St. Lawrence of Brindisi, by B. Vogt, A. Carr, T. Cranny, J. Montalverne, etc.

University of Dayton Review, 5 (Spring, 1968) edited by Norbert Brockman, in memory of Emil Neubert, S.M. (d. 1967), articles by T. Koehler, W.G. Most (Priesthood of Mary), E.D. O'Connor, W. Cole, etc.

University of Dayton Review, 11 (Spring, 1975) for the 30th anniversary of the Dayton Marian Library, papers given fall 1973, e.g., C.J. Brady (Mary and Feminism), A. Schmemann (Mary Archetype of Mankind), W.J. Cole (Mary— An Answer to Woman's Role in the Church), Bishop Joseph L. Bernardin, etc.

GENERAL DISCUSSIONS OF MARIAN DOCTRINE

New Catholic Encyclopedia (1967) and supplementary volumes 16 and 17: most of the entries on Mary are in vol. 9, but check cross-references and index: doctrine, devotion, art, other aspects.

Donald Attwater, *A Dictionary of Mary,* New York, 1956.

Wolfgang Beinert, Mary in the Mystery of Salvation, in *Theology Digest,* 26 (Spring, 1978) 50-53.

Rogatien Bernard, O.P., *The Mystery of Mary,* St. Louis, 1960.

Louis Bouyer, *The Seat of Wisdom,* New York, 1962, also under the title, *Woman and Man with God.* An Essay on the Place of the Virgin Mary in Christian Theology and its Significance for Humanity, London, 1960.

J.B. Carol, *Fundamentals of Mariology;* New York, 1956: basic textbook.

E.R. Carroll, The Mother of Jesus in Catholic Understanding, in *1978 Catholic Almanac,* Huntington, Indiana, 1977; in brief.

J.H. Crehan, article, Mary, in *A Catholic Dictionary of Theology,* vol. 3, 1971, London and Camden, N.J.

Henri Daniel-Rops, *The Book of Mary,* Garden City, N.Y., 1962, pb., chapter "The Heart in the Understanding of Dogma" among good things.

Donal Flanagan of Ireland has written well on our Lady for over twenty years; this is a sampling. *The Theology of Mary,* Cork, 1978, and Butler, Wisconsin, 1978, pb., in series, *Theology Today,* no. 30. "A Future for Marian Theology," in *Ephemerides Mariologicae,* 20 (1970). "The Holy Spirit and Mary's Glory," in *The Furrow,* 24 (October, 1973). "Mary: Belief as Liberation," in *Supplement to Doctrine and Life,* July-August, 1973. "Mother of the Word of Silence," in *Supplement to Doctrine and Life,* March-April, 1974.

R. Garrigou-Lagrange, O.P., *The Mother of the Savior and Our Interior Life,* St. Louis, 1954, and *The Last Writings of R. Garrigou-Lagrange,* New York and London, 1969, chapter on "Devotion to the Blessed Virgin."

Andrew Greeley, *The Mary Myth: On the Femininity of God,* New York, 1977.

Jean Guitton, *The Virgin Mary,* New York, 1952, under title, *The Blessed Virgin,* London, 1952.

Camillus Hay, O.F.M., *Vatican II: Mary's adventure, goal, way,* Australian Catholic Truth Society pamphlet, Melbourne, 1969.

René Laurentin, *Queen of Heaven. A Short Treatise on Marian Theology,* Dublin, London and New York, 1956: this is the second edition of a valuable historical approach to Mariology which has reached a fifth edition in French in 1968; the English is still worthwhile. A different translation into English is in *The Historical and Mystical Christ,* ed. A.M. Henry, O.P. (Theology Library, vol. 5), Chicago, 1958. Also by Laurentin: *The Question of Mary,* New York, 1965, and in pb Techny, Illinois, 1967, the English title is *Mary's Place in the Church,* London, 1965.

George A. Maloney, S.J., *Mary: the Womb of God,* Denville, N.J., 1976, pb.

Charles Moeller, Virgin Mary in Contemporary Thought, and Doctrinal Aspects of Mariology, articles in *Modern Mentality and Evangelization,* Staten Island, N.Y., 1968, vol. 3, originally in *Lumen Vitae,* 8 (April-June, 1953) whole number on The Mother of God.

William G. Most, *Mary in Our Life,* New York, several editions, third was 1959, Image pb was 1963; also by Most, the article on Mary in *Encyclopedia Americana,* vol. 18 (1969).

Heribert Muehlen, New Directions in Mariology, in *Theology Digest,* 24 (Fall, 1976) 286-92.

Alois Mueller, Contemporary Mariology, chapter in *Theology Today,* vol. one, *Renewal in Dogma,* eds. J. Feiner and others, Milwaukee, 1965; also The Basic Principles of Mariology, in *Theology Digest,* 1 (Fall, 1953) 139-44.

S. Napiórkowski, The Present Position in Mariology, in *Concilium,* v. 29 (1967), New York.

Emil Neubert, S.M., *Mary in Doctrine,* Milwaukee, 1954, again as pb Dayton, 1962.

Sister Patricia Noone, *Mary for Today,* Chicago, 1977.

Michael O'Carroll, C.S.Sp., Socia: The Word and the Idea in Regard to Mary, in *Ephemerides Mariologicae,* 25 (1975); given at Rome, May, 1975, at International Mariological Congress.

Jaroslav Pelikan, article, Mary the Mother of Jesus, in *Encyclopedia Brittanica* (1960), vol. 14.

Joseph-Marie Perrin, O.P., *Mary, Mother of Christ and of Christians,* Staten Island, N.Y., 1978, pb.

K. Rahner, *Mary, Mother of the Lord,* New York, 1963; London, 1974, pb.

M. Scheeben, *Mariology,* in two volumes, St. Louis, 1946-47.

E. Schillebeeckx, *Mary, Mother of the Redemption,* New York and London, 1965.

M. Schmaus, the articles on Mariology in both the large *Sacramentum Mundi,* New York, 1969, vol. 3, and *Encyclopedia of Theology. A Concise Sacramentum Mundi,* New York, 1975.

P. Schmidt, *Mary Re-Discovered. An Approach to a Contemporary Mariology,* Melbourne, 1976, pb, English distributor, T. Shand Publications, 221 Golders Green Rd., London.

Federico Suarez, *Our Lady the Virgin,* Chicago, 1959, and pb 1965, also under title *Mary of Nazareth,* Houston, 1973.

Cardinal Suenens, *Mary the Mother of God,* New York,

1959; also *Theology of the Apostolate,* Chicago, 1956, and as pb Techny, Ill., 1962 — on the Legion of Mary pledge.

O.R. Vassall-Phillips, C.SS.R., Mary, Mother of God, in *The Teaching of the Catholic Church,* ed. G. Smith, vol. 1, New York, 1951.

Cyril Vollert, S.J., *A Theology of Mary,* St. Louis, 1965: collected articles.

J. Weiger, *Mary Mother of Faith,* Garden City, N.Y., pb, 1962.

F.M. Willam, *Mary, the Mother of Jesus,* St. Louis, 1954.

MARY IN THE SCRIPTURES

Mary in the New Testament (A collaborative assessment by Protestant, Anglican and Roman Catholic scholars), edited by R.E. Brown, K.P. Donfried, J.A. Fitzmyer and J. Reumann (assisted by eight others), Paulist, New York and Fortress, Philadelphia, Fall, 1978, pb.

Dictionary entries: A. George, S.M., Mary, in X. Léon-Dufour, *Dictionary of Biblical Theology,* New York, 1967, 2nd edition 1973; J. de Fraine, Mary, in L. Hartman, ed., *Encyclopedic Dictionary of the Bible,* New York, 1963; J. Michl, in *Sacramentum Verbi,* ed. J.B. Bauer, vol. 2, 1970, New York; J.J. von Allmen, in his *A Companion to the Bible,* New York, 1958, Mary, under Names (personal).

B.M. Ahern, C.P., *New Horizons,* Notre Dame, Indiana, 1964, pb., Spirit of Old Testament Saints, and Mary, Prototype of the Church.

Horacio Bojorge, S.J., *The Image of Mary According to the Evangelists,* Staten Island, New York 1978, pb.

F.M. Braun, O.P., *Mother of God's People,* Staten Is., N.Y., 1967.

R.E. Brown, S.S., Luke's Method in the Annunciation Narrative, in *No Famine in the Land,* eds. J.W. Flanagan and A. Robinson, Missoula, Mont., 1975; The Meaning of Modern New Testament Studies for an Ecumenical Understanding of Mary, in *Biblical Reflections on Crises Facing the Church,* New York, 1975, pb. Much on our Lady in *The Birth of the Messiah. A Commentary on the Infancy Narratives in Matthew and Luke,* Garden City, N.Y., 1977.

Jean Cantinat, C.M., *Mary in the Bible,* Westminster, Md., 1965.

E.R. Carroll, O.Carm., Pondering the Joyful Mysteries. Reflections on a new book The Birth of the Messiah, in *Our Lady's Digest,* 32 (March-April, 1978) 145-50.

C.P. Ceroke, O.Carm., article, Mary in the Bible, in *New Catholic Encyclopedia* (1967), vol. 9; scholarly in easy-reading style.

R.F. Collins, Mary in the Fourth Gospel: A Decade of Johannine Studies, in *Louvain Studies,* 3 (Fall, 1970); also Mary among Representative Figures of the Fourth Gospel, in *Downside Review,* April, 1976.

W. Dalton, S.J., *Mary in the New Testament,* Melbourne, 1974, pb.

L. Deiss, C.S.Sp., *Daughter of Sion,* Collegeville, Minn., 1972.

A. Feuillet, *Johannine Studies*, Staten Is., N.Y., 1965: Cana and the woman clothed with the sun of the Apocalypse.

Neal Flanagan, O.S.M., Ark of the Covenant, in *Worship*, 35 (May, 1961).

Josephine M. Ford, The Mother of Jesus and the Authorship of the Epistle to the Hebrews, in *The Bible Today*, February, 1976; also Biblical Guidelines to Marian Devotion, in *Review for Religious*, May, 1976.

Jean de Fraine, *Praying with the Bible*, New York, 1964; much on the Magnificat.

Paul Gaechter, S.J., *Light on Mary's Life*, Dublin, 1966.

Jean Galot, S.J., *Mary in the Gospel*, Westminster, Md., 1965.

S. Garofalo, *Mary in the Bible*, Milwaukee, 1961.

A. Gelin, *The Poor of Yahweh*, Collegeville, Minn., 1967, pb., chapter on Mary and Her Song of Poverty.

Jos. A. Grassi, Luke, Theologian of Grace, and Mary, Mother of Jesus, in *The Bible Today*, December, 1970.

G. Graystone and R. Russell, articles, The Mother of Jesus in the Scriptures, and The Brothers of the Lord, in *A New Catholic Commentary on Holy Scripture*, ed. R.C. Fuller and others, London and Camden, N.J., 1969.

T.R. Heath, O.P., Our Lady in Biblical and Speculative Theology, in *The Thomist Reader*, Washington, D.C., 1958.

Alex. Jones, *God's Living Word,* New York, 1965, pb., two chapters on our Lady; also article, The Tool of God, in *Pattern of Scripture,* New York, pb, 1958.

C. Klein (Sister Louis Gabriel), Jewish Women in the Time of Mary of Nazareth, in *The Bible Today,* April, 1972, and in *The Bible Today Reader,* Collegeville, Minn., 1973, pb.

B.J. LeFrois, S.V.D., The Image of Mary in the Scriptures, in *Sisters Today,* January, 1972.

Ernest Lussier, S.S.S., Mariology Post-Vatican II, in *Chicago Studies,* Spring, 1972.

S. Lyonnet, St. Luke's Infancy Narrative, in *Word and Mystery,* ed. Leo O'Donovan, Westminster, Md., 1968.

John McHugh, *The Mother of Jesus in the New Testament,* London and New York, 1975.

C.H. Miller, S.M., Mary and the Old Testament in Vatican II, in *American Ecclesiastical Review,* 163 (December, 1970).

Jerome D. Quinn, Mary, Seat of Wisdom, in *The Bible Today,* April, 1964.

K. Rahner, Take the Child and His Mother, in his book, *Everyday Faith,* New York, 1968: Joseph's hesitation was out of reverent fear.

B. Schepers, O.P., The Holy Remnant and the Immaculate Virgin, in *The Bible Today,* December, 1965.

R. Schnackenburg, *Belief in the New Testament,* New York, 1975, pb., chapter on the Magnificat.

M. Philip Scott, O.C.S.O., The Meaning and Translation of Luke 11:28, in *Irish Theological Quarterly,* 41 (July, 1974): a strong Church sense.

J.R. Sheets, S.J., A Biblical Theology of Mary, in *Review for Religious,* September, 1976.

David Stanley, S.J., *A Modern Scriptural Approach to the Spiritual Exercises,* St. Louis, 1971, pb., with chapters, Our Lady in the Life of the Apostolic Church, Problem of the Infancy Narratives and The Good News of Christmas.

Max Thurian, *Mary Mother of All Christians,* New York, 1964; English title, *Mary Mother of the Lord Figure of the Church,* London, 1963: from the French (1962) by Calvinist monk of Taizé.

Max Zerwick, S.J., The Hour of the Mother, in *The Bible Today,* April, 1965, and also in *Catholic Mind,* June, 1965, and *The Bible Today Reader,* Collegeville, Minn., 1973, pb.: on John 19, 25-27.

TRADITION

Hilda Graef, *Mary, A History of Doctrine and Devotion,* 2 volumes, London and New York, 1963-65; also the single volume, *The Devotion to Our Lady,* New York and London, 1963, of which the title in England was *Devotion to the Blessed Virgin.*

T. Koehler, S.M., "Blessed" from Generation to Generation: Mary in Patristics and in the History of the Church (Outline of an evolving image), in *Seminarium,* 27 (1975).

Luis Díez Merino, C.P., Can Anything Good Come from Nazareth? in *The Bible Today,* Dec., 1973, and Feb., 1974, and The Tomb of Mary, in *The Bible Today,* April, 1974: Holy Land archeology.

Alfred Rush, C.SS.R., "Mors Mariae, vita aeterna": an insight into New Testament apocrypha, in *American Ecclesiastical Review,* 142 (April, 1960) 257-66: early Christian literature on the fate of Mary.

J. Pelikan, Eve or Mary: A test case in the Development of Doctrine, co-published in *The Lamp,* June, 1971, and *The Christian Ministry,* May, 1971.

H. Musurillo, S.J., *Symbolism and the Christian Imagination,* Baltimore, 1962, chapter, Mary: Woman and Virgin.

Robert Murray, S.J., Mary, the Second Eve, in the Early Syriac Fathers, in *Eastern Churches Review,* 3 (Autumn, 1971) 372-84, and in the book *Symbols of Church and Kingdom: A Study in Early Syriac Tradition,* London and New York, 1975.

Hugo Rahner, *Our Lady and the Church,* New York and London, 1961, Chicago, 1965, pb.; see also *Greek Myths and Christian Mystery,* New York, 1963.

Donal Flanagan, Image of the Bride in the Earlier Marian Tradition, in *Irish Theological Quarterly,* 27 (April, 1960) 110-24; Eve in the Writings of Paschasius Radbertus (d.865), in *Irish Theological Quarterly,* 34 (1967).

J.H. Crehan, S.J., Maria Paredros, in *Theological Studies,* 16 (1955) 414-23: image of the bride in early Christian thought.

St. Alphonsus Liguori, *The Glories of Mary,* critical ed., trans. by Chas. G. Fehrenbach, C.SS.R., in 2 volumes, Baltimore, 1962/3.

Charles W. Neumann, S.M., *The Virgin Mary in the Works of St. Ambrose,* Fribourg, Switzerland, 1962: Mary's virginity.

Sr. Benedicta Ward, S.L.G., *The Prayers and Meditations of St. Anselm,* Penguin, pb, Baltimore, 1973: including famous prayers to St. Mary.

Jaroslav Pelikan, *Development of Christian Doctrine: Some Historical Prolegomena,* New Haven, Conn., 1969: Yale lecture on S. Athanasius.

James Good, The Mariology of the Blathmac Poems, in *Irish Ecclesiastical Record,* 104 (July, 1965) 1-7, based on the Jas. Carney discoveries of Gaelic poetry from about the year 700.

Sister Emma T. Healy, S.S.J., *Women According to St. Bonaventure,* Erie, Pa., 1956; much on our Lady.

J.A. Hardon, S.J., Bellarmine and the Queen of Virgins, in *Review for Religious,* 12(1953) 113-21.

Robert Maloy, A Carolingian and Eleventh Century Monastic Sermon on Luke 10: 38-42, in *Marianum,* 38 (1976:4).

Paul-Joseph Hoffer, S.M., *The Spiritual Life according to the Writings of Father Chaminade,* St. Louis, 1969; also on Mary.

John Samaha, S.M., Chaminade's Contribution to Mariology, in *Ephemerides Mariologicae,* 26 (1976).

Sebastian Brock, St. Ephrem on Christ as Light in Mary and in the Jordan, in *Eastern Churches Review,* 7 (1975) 137-44.

Edward D. Carney, O.S.F.S., *The Mariology of St. Francis de Sales,* Newman, Westminster, Md., 1964, distributor.

James S. Langelaan, O.S.F.S., Mary: The Most Beloved and Loving Mother. The Mariology of St. Francis de Sales, in *Marianum,* 38 (1976:3).

H.M. Manteau-Bonamy, O.P., *Immaculate Conception and the Holy Spirit. The Marian Teachings of Father Kolbe,* Kenosha, Wisconsin, 1977, pb., including Pope Paul's homily at the beatification of Blessed Maximilian Kolbe, O.F.M. Conv., Oct. 17,1971.

E. Piacentini, *Immaculate Conception. Panorama of the Marian Doctrine of Blessed M. Kolbe,* Kenosha, Wisconsin, 1975, pamphlet.

John Morson, O.C.S.O., *Christ the Way,* Kalamazoo, Michigan, 1978: on the thought of Guerric of Igny, 12th century Cistercian, one chapter is The Mother of the Word Made Flesh.

Hilary Costello, O.C.S.O., The Mother of Jesus: Our Common Heritage, in *Mt. Carmel* (London), 24 (Winter, 1973) 193-201: on Abbot John of Ford, 12th century English Cistercian.

St. Louis G. de Montfort, *The Love of Eternal Wisdom*

(ed. Somers), Bay Shore, N.Y., 1960; *True Devotion,* many editions, the most common translation is F.W. Faber's of the mid-19th century, though a new one by Malachy G. Carroll was published by Alba, Staten Is., N.Y., 1962, with preface by Frank Duff, founder of the Legion of Mary.

J. Patrick Gaffney, S.M.M., *Mary's Spiritual Maternity according to St. Louis de Montfort,* Bay Shore, N.Y., 1976, both cloth and pb; by Gaffney also, Mary in the Sapiential Spirituality of St. Louis de Montfort, in *Homiletic and Pastoral Review,* 77 (January, 1977) 64-68, and the 3-part series, If Montfort Could Speak Today, in the Montfort magazine (Bay Shore, N.Y.), *Queen,* May-June, July-August and September-October, all 1977.

Michael of St. Augustine, O.Carm. (d. 1684), *Life in and for Mary* (trans. V. Poslusney, O.Carm.), Downers Grove, Ill, 1954, pb., and *Life with Mary. A Treatise on the Marian Life* (trans. T. McGinnis, O.Carm.), New York, 1953, pb.

William J. Cole, S.M., St. Thomas on Mary and Women, in *University of Dayton Review,* Fall, 1975.

T.R. Heath, O.P., *Our Lady* (Summa theologiae, v.51), New York, 1969: St. Thomas' main consideration of the Virgin Mary; see review by E. R. Carroll in *The Thomist,* 24 (1970) 697-701.

J. Gorman, S.M., *William of Newburgh's . . . Commentary on the Canticle of Canticles,* Fribourg, Switzerland, 1960; Gorman translated some selections from this commentary for *Marian Library Studies* (old pamphlet set), no. 99, April, 1963. Marian Library, Dayton, Ohio. William died about 1198.

F. Suarez, S.J., The Dignity and Virginity of the Mother of God, in *The Mysteries of the Life of Christ,* West Baden Springs, Indiana, 1954.

Henri de Lubac, S.J., *The Faith of Teilhard de Chardin,* London, 1965, chapter on the Virgin Mary.

Thomas Corbishley, S.J., *The Spirituality of Teilhard de Chardin,* Glen Rock, N.J., 1972, pb., chapter on our Lady.

John Henry Newman, *Meditations and Devotions,* various editions of this posthumous work, of which part one is Meditations for the Month of May, e.g., Longmans Green Inner Life series, London, 1953; in part in *Blessed Art Thou Among Women,* Denville, N.J., 1977.

F. Friedel, S.M., *The Mariology of Cardinal Newman,* New York, 1928.

Placid Murray, O.S.B., Tower of David: Cardinal Newman's Mariology, in *The Furrow,* 27 (January, 1976) 26-34.

Michael O'Carroll, C.S.Sp., Our Lady in Newman and Vatican II, in *Downside Review,* 89 (January, 1971).

PARTICULAR DOCTRINES

Divine Motherhood

C. Feckes, *The Mystery of the Divine Motherhood,* New York, 1941.

A. Vonier, O.S.B., *The Divine Motherhood,* in *Collected Works,* vol. 1, Westminster, Md., 1952.

E. Mersch, S.J., *The Theology of the Mystical Body,* St. Louis, 1951, chapter, Mary, Mother of Jesus.

Mary's Virginity

R.E. Brown, S.S., *The Virginal Conception and Bodily Resurrection of Jesus,* New York, 1973, pb., also London.

Alan Clark, The Virgin Birth: A Theological Appraisal, in *Theological Studies,* 34 (Dec., 1973) 576-93: on the virginity in bringing forth Jesus, *virginitas in partu.*

John F. Craghan, C.SS.R., Mary, the Virginal Wife and the Married Virgin, in *The Bible Today,* April, 1968, also Mary's 'ante partum' virginity: the Biblical View, in *American Ecclesiastical Review,* June, 1970, on the virginal conception of Jesus.

Joseph Fitzmyer, S.J., The Virginal Conception of Jesus in the New Testament, in *Theological Studies,* 34 (1973) 541-75; see reply by R.E. Brown, Luke's Description of the Virginal Conception, in *Theological Studies,* 35 (1974) 360-62.

M. Miguens, O.F.M., *The Virgin Birth,* Westminster, Md., 1975; see also, Mary a Virgin? Alleged Silence in the New Testament, in *Marian Studies,* 26 (1975).

Michael O'Carroll, C.S.Sp., The Virginal Conception. Some Recent Problems, in *Marianum,* 37 (1975).

John A. Sabila, S.J., The Virgin-Birth Debate in Anthropological Literature, in *Theological Studies,* 36 (Sept., 1975).

John R. Sheets, S.J., Virginal Conception—Fact and Faith, in *Chicago Studies,* 14 (Fall, 1975) 279-96.

Joseph Ratzinger, *Introduction to Christianity,* New York, 1970; chapter on "conceived by the Holy Spirit, born of the Virgin Mary."

Immaculate Conception

A. Bonnar, Eadmer: De conceptione sanctae Mariae, in *Irish Ecclesiastical Record,* 90 (December, 1958) 378-91, article, in English, on the defense of the Immaculate Conception by the English monk Eadmer, who died early in the 12th century.

J. Bonnefoy, O.F.M., *The Immaculate Conception in the Divine Plan,* Paterson, N.J., 1967.

J.B. Carol, O.F.M., *A History of the Controversy over the "debitum peccati,"* St. Bonaventure, N.Y., 1978, pb; can our Lady be said to have fallen in any sense under the universal law of sin, even though immaculately conceived; the author favors total exemption, and surveys positions pro and con.

T.W. Coyle, C.SS.R., Historical Development of the Dogma of the Immaculate Conception, in *Proceedings of the Ninth Convention of the Catholic Theological Society of America,* 1954.

J. Hennesey, S.J., A Prelude to Vatican I: American Bishops and the Definition of the Immaculate Conception, in *Theological Studies,* 25 (1964) 409-19.

A. Hulsbosch, O.S.A., *God in Creation and Evolution,* New York, 1966, chapter, The Mother of God.

Robert Kress, A Feast for the Broken-Hearted, in *The Sign,* Dec. 1976/January, 1977.

S. Mathews, S.M., editor, *The Promised Woman; An Anthology of the Immaculate Conception,* St. Meinrad, Indiana, 1954: Sheen, Giordani, Hoelle, R.A. Knox, and key documents.

Herbert McCabe, O.P., The Immaculate Conception, in *Doctrine and Life,* 25 (December, 1975) 869-74.

E.D. O'Connor, C.S.C., editor, *The Dogma of the Immaculate Conception,* Notre Dame, Indiana, 1958: C. Journet, G. Jouassard, F. Dvornik, C. Balic, R. Laurentin, M. Vloberg (art), plus extended bibliography; by O'Connor, article, Immaculate Conception, in *Catholic Dictionary of Theology,* vol. 2, 1967, London and Camden, N.J.

K. Rahner, S.J., The Immaculate Conception, in *Theological Investigations,* vol. 1, London and Baltimore, 1961; also The Dogma of the Immaculate Conception in Our Spiritual Life, in *Theological Investigations,* vol. 3, 1967.

A. Vanneste, *The Dogma of Original Sin,* Atlantic Highlands, N.J., 1975, chapter, The Immaculate Conception and Our Lady.

Assumption

W.J. Burghardt, S.J., *The Testimony of the Patristic Age Concerning Mary's Death,* Westminster, Md., 1957, pb, also in *Marian Studies,* 8 (1957).

J. Crehan, The Assumption and the Jerusalem Liturgy, in *Theological Studies,* 30 (1969) 312-25.

J. Duhr, S.J., *The Glorious Assumption of the Mother of God,* New York, 1950.

Donal Flanagan, Eschatology and the Assumption, in *Concilium,* v. 41 (1969).

Rosemary Haughton, Mary's Body is Bread, Too, in *The Sign,* November, 1976.

J.P. Kenny, S.J., The Assumption of Mary: Its Relevance for Us Today, in *Clergy Review,* 63 (1978) 289-294.

Robert Kress, Mary's Assumption, God's Promise Fulfilled, in *America,* August 20, 1977.

Bernard Lonergan, S.J., The Assumption and Theology, in *Collection,* ed. by F.E. Crowe, New York, 1967; an essay first out in 1948.

Walter Ong, S.J., The Lady and the Issue, in Ong's *In the Human Grain,* New York, 1966: reprint of an essay from the time of the Assumption definition.

K. Rahner, The Interpretation of the Dogma of the Assumption, in *Theological Investigations,* vol. 1, London and Baltimore, 1961; also Mary's Assumption, a sermon, in *Opportunities for Faith. Elements of a Modern Spirituality,* New York, 1974.

The Thomist, issue on the Assumption, 14 (January, 1951): Bishop Sheen, G. Roschini, K.J. Healy, O.Carm., J.B. Carol, etc.

Thought, 26 (Winter, 1951/52): Three Studies on the Assumption, by M.V. O'Connell, J.L. Tyne and R.W. Gleason.

S.Mathews, S.M., editor, *Queen of the Universe,* St.
Meinrad, Indiana, 1957, anthology of queenship and
Assumption: papal documents and articles by T.B. Falls,
M. Philipon, W.G. Most, etc.

Mediation of Mary

J.B. Carol, in *Ephemerides Mariologicae,* 26 (1976),
taking part in a discussion on the mediation.

W.G. Most, in *Ephemerides Mariologicae,* 26 (1976),
part of the same discussion, takes issue with editor Alonso.

Michael O'Carroll, C.S.Sp., Vatican II and Our Lady's
Mediation, in *Irish Theological Quarterly,* January, 1970.

G.D. Smith, *Mary's Part in Our Redemption,* 2nd ed.,
New York, 1954.

Mary-Church Relationship

Barbara Albrecht, Mary: Type and Model of the Church,
in *Review for Religious,* 36 (July, 1977) 517-24.

Hans Urs von Balthasar, *Church and World,* New York,
1967, much on Mary; *Word and Redemption,* New York,
1965, the chapter, Spirituality.

Y. Congar, What "type" meant to the Fathers, in *Theology
Digest,* 7 (Winter, 1959) 27-28.

Richard Kugelman, C.P., The Hebrew Concept of Corpo-
rate Personality and Mary, the type of the Church, in *Maria
in sacra Scriptura,* vol. 6, proceedings of the Santo Domingo
international Mariological Congress, 1965, proceedings published Rome, 1967, 179-84.

Henri de Lubac, S.J., *Splendor of the Church,* New York and London, also pb., 1963, chapter, The Church and Our Lady: and some pages in the address, Lumen Gentium and the Fathers, in both his book, *The Church: Paradox and Mystery,* Staten Is., N.Y., 1969, and in *Vatican II: An Interfaith Appraisal,* ed. J. Miller, Notre Dame, Indiana 1966.

G.A. Maloney, S.J., Mary and the Church as seen by the early Fathers, in *Diakonia,* 9 (1974:1); A New but Ancient Mariology, in *Diakonia,* 8 (1973) 303-5.

N.D. O'Donoghue, O.C.D., Mary and the Church, in *What is the Church?* ed. by D. Flanagan, New York and Dublin, 1962.

K. Rahner, Mary and the Church, in his *Spiritual Exercises,* New York, 1965.

Otto Semmelroth, S.J., *Mary, Archetype of the Church,* New York, 1963, preface by J. Pelikan.

John Thornhill, S.M., The Mystery of Mary and the Church, in *Homiletic and Pastoral Review,* 67 (1966) 31-40.

The Holy Spirit and Mary

S. Falvo, With Mary in the Cenacle, in his book, *The Hour of the Holy Spirit,* Athlone, Ireland, 1975, pb.

R. Laurentin, *Catholic Pentecostalism,* Garden City, N.Y., 1977, chapter on our Lady.

Kilian McDonnell, O.S.B., Protestants, Pentecostals and Mary. Does Mary Belong Just to Catholics?, in *New Covenant,* March, 1977.

G.A. Maloney, Do not be Afraid to Take Mary Home, in *Catholic Charismatic,* October-November, 1976.

G.T. Montague, S.M. *Riding the Wind,* Ann Arbor, Mich., 1974, pb., now as a Pillar Book, Harcourt, Brace & Jovanovich, New York, 1977, pb; the chapter, Mary and Learning the Ways of the Spirit, was also in *Our Lady's Digest,* March-April, 1975; Mary's Gift for God's People, A Scriptural View, in *New Covenant,* May, 1975.

E.D. O'Connor, C.S.C., *Pope Paul and the Spirit, Charisms and Church Renewal in the Teaching of Paul VI,* Notre Dame, Indiana, 1978, cloth and pb., documents and commentary.

Louis Pfaller and Larry J. Alberts, *Mary is Pentecostal,* Pecos, N.M., 1973, pamphlet.

Cardinal Suenens, *A New Pentecost?,* New York, 1977, pb., chapter on our Lady.

Mary and Ecumenism

Ada Mary Ammon, The Joy of Mary, in *Jesus Caritas* (Charles of Jesus Association), England, Winter, 1970; by Methodist member of the Ecumenical Society of the B.V.M.

C.V. LaFontaine, S.A., A Protestant Episcopal Contribution to Roman Mariology, in *Marianum,* 39 (1977); LaFontaine with C. Angell, *Prophet of Reunion,* New York, 1975, biography of Paul James Francis Wattson, with comment by T. Cranny, Prophet or Trickster? in *Homiletic and Pastoral Review,* 76 (July, 1976), 75-76.

J.E. Barnes, A Caroline Devotion to the Virgin Mary, in *Theology* (London), 73 (December, 1970); Mariology of

Bishop Kent and Lumen Gentium: A Comparison of Caroline and Conciliar Principles, in *Heythrop Journal,* 13 (July, 1972) 298-306; editor of *Devotions of Our Lady from Anglican Writers of the 17th Century,* London, 1973, pb.

Karl Barth, *Ad limina apostolorum,* Richmond, Va., 1968, with A Letter about Mariology.

Cardinal Bea, Mariology and Ecumenism, in *Catholic Mind,* 64 (May, 1966) 36-44, and in different translation in *Way to Unity After the Council,* New York, 1966.

S. Benko, *Protestants, Catholics and Mary,* Valley Forge, Pa., 1968; reviews by E.R. Carroll in *Salesian Studies* (Hyattsville, Md.) 6 (Summer, 1969) 115-118, and by C. Vollert in *Theological Studies,* 30 (December, 1969) 722-724; by Benko also, An Intellectual History of Changing Protestant Attitudes towards Mariology between 1950 and 1967, in *Ephemerides Mariologicae,* 24 (1974).

G.C. Berkouwer, *The Second Vatican Council and the New Catholicism,* Grand Rapids, Mich., 1965, chapter, Mary.

Sergius Bulgakov: A Bulgakov Anthology, editors James Pain and N. Zernov, Philadelphia and London, 1976, chapter The Burning Bush.

E.R. Carroll, A Waldensian View on the Virgin Mary, in *American Ecclesiastical Review,* 135 (December 1956), on G. Miegge's book, *The Virgin Mary;* also by Carroll, The Mary-Church Analogy in Ecumenical Dialogue: Agreements and Disagreements, in *Acta congressus internationalis de theologia concilii Vaticani II,* Rome, 1968, 245-254, from

Roman congress of 1966; and Our Lady and Ecumenical Hope, in *Queen* (Montfort Fathers), 27 (November-December, 1976), the thought of J.C. de Satgé.

Y. Congar, O.P., *Christ, Our Lady and the Church,* London and Westminster, Md., 1957, correctly acclaimed as a classic on differences between Protestants and Catholics; Mary and the Church in Protestantism, in his book, *Dialogue Between Christians,* Westminster, Md., 1966.

G.M. Corr, O.S.M., "Mother of the Church" an Ecumenical Title?, in *Clergy Review,* August, 1976, also in *Marianum* 37 (1975).

Abbé P. Couturier introduces a Dialogue on our Lady, in *Our Lady's Digest,* May-June, 1972.

T. Cranny, S.A., *Our Lady and Reunion,* Graymoor, N.Y., 1962, and *Is Mary Relevant? A Commentary on Ch. 8 of Lumen Gentium the Constitution on the Church,* New York, 1970.

B. de Margerie, S.J., Dogmatic Development by Abridgement or Concentration? in *Marian Studies,* 27 (1976) 64-92, from the French, with an appendix in reply to A. Dulles' address, A Proposal to Lift Anathemas, in *Origins: N.C. Documentary Service,* December 26, 1974.

John C. deSatgé, *Down to Earth: The New Protestant Vision of the Virgin Mary,* Wilmington, N.C., 1976, cloth and pb; the English edition, London, 1976, titled *Mary and the Christian Gospel.*

G. Ebeling, The Mariological Dogma, in *The Word of God and Tradition: Historical Studies Interpreting the*

Divisions of Christianity, Philadelphia, 1968, essay from time of Assumption definition.

Austin Farrer, Mary, Scripture and Tradition, in *Interpretation and Belief*, London, 1976, ed. by C.C. Conti; previously published in the Mascall and Box edited *The Blessed Virgin Mary: Essays by Anglican Writers* (London, 1963), but here also Conti's introduction and Farrer's article, Infallibility and Historical Revelation.

J. Feiner and L. Vischer, editors, *The Common Catechism*, New York, 1975; R. Laurentin collaborated on the Marian materials.

G. Finazzo, The Virgin Mary in the Koran, in *L'Osservatore Romano*, English weekly, April 13, 1978.

D. Flanagan, Luther on the Magnificat, in *Ephemerides Mariologicae*, 24 (1974); also Postscript to Lumen gentium, chapter eight, in *Irish Theological Quarterly*, 38 (January, 1971) 67-71; Mary in the Ecumenical Discussion, in *Irish Theological Quarterly*, 40 (July, 1973) 227-49; Marian Theology in the Ecumenical Discussion, in *Irish Theological Quarterly*, 33 (1966) 352-57, on a book by Brandenburg.

Neal Flanagan, O.S.M., A Marian Creed, in *The Bible Today*, December, 1974, and The Mother of the Lord, an Ecumenical Presence, in *Marianum*, 37 (1975).

G. Florovsky, The Ever-Virgin Mother of God, in Collected Works, vol. 3, *Creation and Redemption*, Belmont, Mass. 1976.

R.H. Fuller, The Role of Mary in Anglicanism, in *Worship*, 51 (May, 1977) 214-24, review and reaction to de Satgé's book, *Down to Earth: The New Protestant Vision of the Virgin Mary*.

Elsie Gibson, Mary and the Protestant Mind, in *Review for Religious*, 24 (May, 1965) 389-98.

Charles Gray-Stack, "The Most Holy Birth-giver of God," in *Doctrine and Life*, 27 (January, 1977) 40-50, from 13th Glenstal ecumenical conference, 1976, by an Anglican.

J.M. Haire, Born of the Virgin Mary, in *Doctrine and Life*, August, 1976, also from Glenstal conference, Presbyterian view.

Toivo Harjunpaa, A Lutheran View of Mariology, in *America*, 117 (Oct. 21, 1967) 436-7, 440-1.

A.G. Hebert, S.S.M., The Virgin Mary as the Daughter of Zion, in *Theology* (London), 53 (November, 1950) 403-10.

Walter J. Hollenweger, Ave Maria: Mary, the Reformers and the Protestants, in *One in Christ*, 13 (1977) 185-90.

Otto Karrer, S.J., The Image of Mary, in *The Kingdom of God Today*, New York, 1965.

J.N.D. Kelly, *Early Christian Doctrines*, New York and London, 5th edition, 1978, pb., chapter, Mary and the Saints.

A. Kniazeff, The Great Sign of the Heavenly Kingdom and Its Advent in Strength, in *St. Vladimir's Theological Quarterly*, 13 (1969) 53-75: our Lady in Orthodox liturgical piety.

A. Lancashire, *Born of the Virgin Mary,* London, 1962.

John Lawson, Mariology: An Irenic Statement from a Protestant, in *Worship,* 41 (1967) 211-21, English Methodist who has written on St. Irenaeus.

V. Lossky, Panagia, in collected papers, *In the Image and Likeness of God,* eds. J.H. Erickson and T.E. Bird, Crestwood, N.Y., 1974.

Andrew Louth, *Mary and the Mystery of the Incarnation.* An Essay on the Mother of God in the Theology of Karl Barth, Oxford, 1977: originally a paper to the Ecumenical Society of the B.V.M., October, 1976.

J.A. Ross Mackenzie, A Protestant Discusses Mary, in *Origins: N.C. Documentary Service,* December 29, 1977, and under the speaker's original title, a phrase from John Calvin, Let Us Now Learn to Praise the Holy Virgin, in *Our Lady's Digest,* May-June, 1978: on receiving the president's patronal medal at the Catholic University of America, Dec. 7, 1977.

John Macquarrie, *Christian Unity and Diversity,* London and Philadelphia, 1975, pb., chapter on Mary.

E.L. Mascall and H.S. Box, editors, *The Blessed Virgin Mary: Essays by Anglican Writers,* London, 1963; E.L. Mascall, editor, *The Mother of God,* London, 2nd printing, 1959, by various authors, Anglican and Orthodox.

Donald Nicholson, Mary: A Living Tradition in Anglicanism, in *Clergy Review,* 62 (August, 1977) 318-23.

Heiko Oberman, *The Virgin Mary in Evangelical Perspec-*

tive, Philadelphia, 1971, pb, with an introduction for this edition by T.F. O'Meara, O.P.; originally an article in *Journal of Ecumenical Studies,* 1 (1964) 271-98.

T.O'Meara, O.P., *Mary in Protestant and Catholic Theology,* New York, 1966.

Paul Palmer, S.J., Mary in Protestant Theology and Worship, in *Theological Studies,* 15 (1954) 519-541.

Warren Quanbeck, Problems of Mariology, in *Dialogue on the Way,* ed. by G. Lindbeck, Minneapolis, 1965.

Herbert W. Richardson, Mother of the Church: A Protestant Point of View in *Ephemerides Mariologicae,* 27 (1977), reprinted from a 1965 article, see one-page condensation in *Theology Digest,* 14 (Spring, 1966) 60; on Richardson's thought see E.R. Carroll, Mariology and Theology Today, in *Ephemerides Mariologicae,* 20 (1970) 137-151.

Charles Schleck, C.S.C., Mary and Ecumenism, in *Thought,* 41 (1966) 523-44.

Edmund Schlink, *The Coming Christ and the Coming Church,* Philadelphia, 1968, written after first session of the Council, material on Mary.

Roger Schutz, A Calvinist Monk Reflects on Luther and our Lady, in *Our Lady's Digest,* March-April, 1976.

Polycarp Sherwood, O.S.B., Byzantine Mariology, in *Proceedings of the Catholic Theological Society of America,* 15 (1960) 107-134.

J.R. Sibley, The Meaning of Mary for Modern Man, in

Religion in Life, 45 (Summer, 1976) 174-83, a Methodist magazine.

L. Gordon Tait, Karl Barth and the Virgin Mary, in *Journal of Ecumenical Studies,* 4 (1967) 406-25.

Geoffrey Wainwright, Mary in Relation to the Doctrinal and Spiritual Emphases of Methodism, in *One in Christ,* 11 (April, 1975) 121-144.

Gordon S. Wakefield, The Virgin Mary in Methodism, in *One in Christ,* 4 (1968) 156-164.

J. Neville Ward, *Five for Sorrow, Ten for Joy,* London and Garden City, N.Y., 1973, also pb 1974, rosary meditations by a Methodist pastor; and chapter, Belonging, in *Friday Afternoon: The Seven Last Words,* London, 1976, pb.

Edward J. Yarnold, S.J., Marian Dogmas and Reunion, in *The Month,* June, 1971.

Liturgy

Mary in the Liturgy, 15th National Liturgical Week, 1954, Elsberry, Mo., 1955: B. Ahern, J. Hofinger, G. Sloyan.

G.G. Meersseman, ed., *The Akathist Hymn,* Fribourg, Switzerland, 1958; *Four Akathistos Hymns in Honor of the Mother of God,* published in France, 1975, to be had from St. Vladimir's Crestwood, N.Y.; *Office of the Akathist,* by E.F. James, Bay Shore, N.Y., 1959, pamphlet.

Andrew Chao and Paul Brunner, *Glory to the Lord, 20 Bible Vigils,* Collegeville, Minn., 1966, pb, six on Mary.

L. Dannemiller, *Bible Devotions in honor of Mary, the Mother of God,* New York, 1962, pamphlet.

G. Diekmann, O.S.B., Mary Model of Our Worship, in book *Come Let Us Worship,* Baltimore, 1961, pb 1966; was in *Worship,* 34 (October, 1960).

F.X. Durrwell, C.SS.R., *In the Redeeming Christ,* New York, 1963, chapter, Mary Amongst Us.

Robert F. Hoey, S.M., *The Experimental Liturgy Book,* New York, 1969, has J.J. Kaufmann, A Marian Liturgy.

R. Laurentin, Mary in the Liturgy and in Catholic Devotion, in *The Furrow,* 17 (1966) 343-65; *Our Lady and the Mass,* New York, 1959.

Thomas Merton, A Homily on Light and the Virgin Mary, in *Seasons of Celebration.* Meditations on the Cycle of Liturgical Feasts, New York, 1965; also The Woman Clothed with the Sun, chapter in *New Seeds of Contemplation,* New York, 1961, and Electa ut sol, chapter in *Seeds of Contemplation,* Norfolk, Conn. 1949.

Norman Perry, O.F.M., Bible Service to Honor Mary, in *St. Anthony Messenger,* May, 1969, can be had as fold-out leaflet.

H.A. Reinhold, Mary in the Liturgy, in *Jubilee,* 13 (February, 1966) 10-13.

Catechetics

E.R. Carroll, Mariology, in *An American Catholic Catechism,* ed. G. Dyer, New York, 1975, cloth and pb, first in

Chicago Studies, Fall, 1973; Preaching the Good News about the Mother of Jesus, in *Homiletic and Pastoral Review,* October, 1972; The Mother of Jesus in the Communion of Saints–Challenge to the Churches (presidential address), in *Proceedings of the Catholic Theological Society of America,* 21 (1966) 249-65.

In *The Catechist,* 8 (May, 1975): Mary Ann Clark and Jerri Pogue, Mary: Model for All Believers (workshop), and C. Thomas Moore, O.P., Mary's Pilgrimage of Faith, with editorial by Patricia Fischer.

John A. Hardon, *The Catholic Catechism. A Contemporary Catechism of the Teachings of the Catholic Church,* Garden City, N.Y., 1975, pb., section five on our Lady.

James B. Hawker, Mary Speaks to the Catechist, in *Today's Catholic Teacher,* 11 (May, 1978) 18-19.

J. Hofinger, chapter, Mary's Significance for the Religion Teacher, in his book *You Are My Witnesses: Spirituality for Religion Teachers,* Huntington, Indiana, 1977, pb.

F.M. Jelly, O.P., two chapters, The Mother of Jesus, and Mary, Mother and Model of the Church, in T.C. Lawler, D. Wuerl and R. Lawler, O.F.M. Cap., editors, *The Teaching of Christ. A Catholic Catechism for Adults,* Huntington, Indiana, 1976, cloth and paperback; there is also a guide, *The Teaching of Christ: A Study Guide,* Huntington, 1977, pb: from Fr. Jelly further, Mary and the Eucharistic Liturgy, in *Cross and Crown,* December, 1967.

Devotions: Immaculate Heart, Rosary, Appearances of Our Lady

A Heart for All. The Immaculate Heart of Mary in the Apparitions of Fatima, a symposium, Washington, N.J. 1972, L. Ciappi, O.P., J.M. Alonso, C.M.F., and others.

K.J. Healy, O.Carm., Theology of the Doctrine of the Immaculate Heart of Mary, in *Proceedings of the Catholic Theological Society of America,* 4 (1949) 102-127.

H. Keller, S.J., *The Heart of Mary,* Dublin, 1950, Baltimore, reprint in the 1970's.

T. Sparks, O.P., Reparation to the Immaculate Heart of Mary, in *From An Abundant Spring* (W. Farrell memorial volume of *The Thomist),* New York, 1952.

Fred Bergewisch, S.J., A Rosary for Our Times, in *St. Anthony Messenger,* October, 1969, also as pamphlet.

W.J. Harrington, O.P., *Rosary, Gospel Prayer,* Staten Is., N.Y., 1975.

Rosemary Haughton, *Feminine Spirituality: Reflections on the Mysteries of the Rosary,* New York, 1975, pb.

Patrick Peyton, C.S.C., *All for Her,* Garden City, N.Y., 1967, pb 1974; by apostle of the family Rosary.

The Pilgrim Virgin's Scripture-based Home Visitation Program, Bay Shore, N.Y., 1976, large-size pamphlet from the Legion of Mary, Los Angeles.

John Delaney, ed, *A Woman Clothed with the Sun,* Garden City, N.Y., 1960, pb. also: eight apparitions.

J.S. Kennedy, *Light on the Mountain,* Garden City, N.Y., 1965, pb, story of LaSalette, 1846.

D. Demarest and C. Taylor, editors, *The Dark Virgin, The Book of Our Lady of Guadalupe,* Fresno, California, 1956.

A Handbook on Guadalupe, Kenosha, Wisconsin, 1974, pb, by various authors, including Dr. Charles Wahlig, demostrating the images in the eye of the Virgin on Juan Diego's tilma.

P. Wallace Platt, C.S.B., *Church Art and Architecture, Faith Abounding. The New Basilica of Our Lady of Guadalupe Mexico City,* in *Clergy Review,* 63 (March, 1978) 109-112.

Virgil Elizondo, Our Lady of Guadalupe as a Cultural Symbol: "The Power of the Powerless," in *Concilium,* v. 112, (1977).

E.J. Melvin, C.M., The Miraculous Medal and Sacred Scripture, in *The Priest,* December, 1977.

Alan Neame, *The Happening at Lourdes: The sociology of the Grotto,* New York and London, 1967.

Odile de Montfort and John O'Meara, *Ordeal at Lourdes: the New Discoveries,* New York and London, 1960.

R. Laurentin, *Meaning of Lourdes,* Dublin, 1959.

R. Laurentin, The Persistence of Popular Piety, in *Concilium,* v. 81 (1973).

Bishop O'Dwyer, Nature and Grace at Lourdes, in *Catholic Mind,* December 1977.

Bishop W. Rubin, Aspects of Popular Piety in the Church of Silence, in *World Mission,* 28 (Fall, 1977, and Winter, 1977/8).

Marion A. Habig, O.F.M., *The Franciscan Crown,* Chicago, 1976: rosary of the seven joys of our Lady: also by Habig, *Saints of the Americas,* Huntington, Indiana, 1974, with part two on the Marian history of America.

A Marian Bicentennial Calendar in the U.S.A., in English *L'Osservatore Romano,* December 11, 1975.

Devotional, Womanhood, Priestly Life, and Miscellany

C. Boxer,O.P., Epilogue: A Sermon on the gospel for Our Lady of the Snows, in *Christians and World Freedom,* ed. L. Bright, London, 1966, pb.

W.J. Burghardt, S.J., The Place of Mary in Today's Church, in *Catholic Mind,* 56 (1968) 27-31.

Sidney Callahan, *The Magnificat: The Prayer of Mary,* New York, 1975, pb, classic prayer series.

A. Cameron-Brown, O.S.B., Winter Rose, in *New Black-friars,* 50 (December, 1969) 789-91.

Carlo Carretto, *The God Who Comes,* Maryknoll, N.Y., 1974, and pb., New York, 1976; final chapter on BV.

G.K. Chesterton, Mary and the Convert, in *Marianum,* 37 (1975), with author's corrections; for a letter of Belloc to Chesterton of December 11, 1907, see Eugene F. Shaw, A December Letter for May, in *America,* May 3, 1975.

Thomas F. Clarke, S.J., Mary: Pilgrimage and Celebration, in *Catholic Mind,* November, 1969.

Robert Faricy, S.J., *Spirituality for Religious Life,* New York, 1976, pb, chapter on Mary.

James J. Flood, *To Preach, To Teach, To Pray: Mary,* Washington, D.C., 1975, pb, for current feasts in the calendar.

Bernard Haering, C.J.S.R., *Mary and Your Everyday Life,* Liguori, Missouri, 1978, cloth and pb, English edition is *The Song of the Servant,* London, 1977.

J.C. Haughey, S.J., *Should Anyone Say Forever,* Garden City, N.Y., cloth, 1975, pb, 1977: Much On Mary in ch. five.

T. Heath, O.P., Our Lady as Friend, in *The Sign,* June 1973.

Bishop Gerard Huyghe, *Growth in the Holy Spirit,* Westminster, Md., 1966; on Mary's faith, 47-100.

Robert Kress, Mariology and the Christian's Self-concept, in *Review for Religious,* 31 (May, 1972) 414-419.

Jacques Loew, *Face to Face with God. The Bible's Way to Prayer,* London, 1977, pb, and New York, cloth, 1978; chapter, Praying with Mary.

Floyd A. Lotito, O.F.M., I Never Said Goodbye to Mary,

in *Our Lady's Digest,* January-Febraury, 1976.

John W. Lynch, *A Woman Wrapped in Silence,* New York, 1975, first paperback edition of famous book-length poem that went through many editions in cloth.

Enda McDonough, The Role of Mary, in *The Furrow,* 25 (September, 1974) 488-93, from the shrine of Our Lady of Knock.

J. Moltmann, *Gospel of Liberation,* Waco, Texas, 1973, chapter on Magnificat.

M. Basil Pennington, O.C.S.O., *Daily We Touch Him,* Garden City, N.Y., 1977, has chapter, Mary. The Faithfull Woman.

Arturo Paoli, *Freedom to Be Free,* Maryknoll, N.Y., 1973, has chapter, The Free Woman, was an article in *Maryknoll* magazine, Maÿ, 1971, Mary, A Woman for Our Times; also *Meditations on Saint Luke,* Maryknoll, N.Y., 1977, cloth and pb, with chapter, The Children of the Desert.

Patrick H. Reardon (Anglican), The Bible, The Soul and the Mother of Jesus, in *Review for Religious,* 32 (July, 1973) 829-33.

Archbishop Raya, *The Face of God: An Introduction to Eastern Spirituality,* Denville, N.J., 1976, chapter, Mary Theotokos.

Jean Roche, S.J., *The Blessed Virgin's Silence,* Denville, N.J., 1965, preface by John W. Lynch.

Fulton J. Sheen, *The World's Great Love: The Prayer of the Rosary,* New York, 1978. in the Seabury Classic Prayer series; earlier titled *The World's First Love,* Garden City, N.Y., pb, original cloth, 1952.

Herbert F. Smith, S.J., *The Lord Experience,* Collegeville, Minn., 1973, chapter, Thoughts About Mary.

Sister Joan Noreen Testa, The Role of Mary in a World of Many Hungers, in *Dimension,* 9 (Winter, 1977) 144-50.

P.G. van Breemen, S.J., *Called by Name,* Denville, N.J., cloth, 1976, pb, 1978, chapter on Mary.

A Woman for All Seasons, Edward Wakin interviews Fr. Eamon R. Carroll, O.Carm., in *U.S. Catholic,* 43 (May, 1978).

John Cardinal Wright, The Cult of Mary in the Age of the Cult of the Flesh, in *The Church: Hope of the World,* ed. by D.W. Wuerl, Kenosha, Wisconsin, 1972.

R. Laurentin, Mary and Womanhood in the Renewal of Christian Anthropology, in *Marian Library Studies,* 1 (1969).

Edward J. Farrell, *Can You Drink This Cup?,* Denville, N.J., 1978, chapter on Mary and the Liberation of Women.

Pat Driscoll, Daring to Grow, in book *Women in a Strange Land,* edited by C.B. Fischer, B. Brenneman and A.M. Bennett, Philadelphia, 1975, pb, on Mary as model of modern women.

Mary Reed Newland, Mary and Liberation, in *The Living Light,* Summer, 1971.

Paul Philippe, O.P., *The Blessed Virgin and the Priesthood,* Chicago, 1955.

K. Rahner, Mary and the Apostolate, in book *The Christian Commitment,* New York, 1964.

Fulton J. Sheen, *Those Mysterious Priests,* Garden City, N.Y., 1974, dedicated to our Lady, two chapters on her.

H.C. Gardiner, S.J., Our Lady in Literature, in *Catholic Mind,* 59 (November-December, 1961) 506-10.

Vincent Cronin, *Mary Portrayed,* London, 1968: Our Lady in art.

Geoffrey Turner, Mythology and Marian Dogma, in *New Blackfriars,* 54 (July, 1973) 303-313.

Vera von der Heydt, *Prospects for the Soul. Soundings in Jungian Psychology and Religion,* London, 1976, pb, chapter, Psychological Implications of the Dogma of the Assumption.